BLACK BELT®
P R E S E N T S
THE BEST OF
BILL WALLACE

BLACK BELT®
P R E S E N T S
THE BEST OF
BILL WALLACE

Compiled by Jon Thibault

Edited by Raymond Horwitz
and Jon Thibault

Graphic Design by John Bodine

Front and Back Cover Photos by Rick Hustead

©2005 Black Belt Communications LLC

All Rights Reserved

Printed in the United States of America

Library of Congress Control Number: 2005902084

ISBN 0-89750-146-2

First Printing 2005

WARNING

BLACK BELT BOOKS
A Division of OHARA ⊞ PUBLICATIONS, INC.
World Leader in Martial Arts Publications

Photo by Rick Hustead

ABOUT THE AUTHOR

Bill "Superfoot" Wallace earned his nickname by winning 23 consecutive kickboxing bouts as the Professional Karate Association (PKA) middleweight champion. He is a world-renown educator, lecturer and author whose popular columns for *Black Belt* have been gathered here for the first time.

Wallace began studying karate in 1967 after a leg injury prevented him from practicing judo, his first martial art. Though he was unable to kick with his right leg, he excelled in karate and competed in tournaments across the country, capturing virtually every major title on the tournament circuit and garnering multiple wins at the U.S. Championships, the USKA Grand Nationals and the Top 10 Nationals.

When Wallace entered the fledgling sport of kickboxing in 1974, a legend was born. At his first international competition in Germany, he punched and kicked his way through his opponents and was declared the world champion. Wallace was twice inducted into the *Black Belt* Hall of Fame as 1977's Competitor of the Year and 1978's Man of the Year.

Wallace retired as the undefeated PKA middleweight champion in 1980. He teaches seminars all over the world and remains one of the most respected personalities in martial arts. Wallace lives with his wife in Florida.

TABLE OF CONTENTS

Part 2: Personal History

Part 3: Commentary

FOREWORD

Thank you for buying this book. These are my views on techniques, psychology, physiology and everything else relevant to martial arts training. Like all advice, you should take mine with a grain of salt, but keep in mind that I've reached my conclusions not only through personal trial and error but also by exchanging ideas with some of the most revered and well-known martial arts masters, instructors and fighters in the world.

Sometimes people get mad at me and say I'm wrong about this or that, but my columns for *Black Belt* magazine are basically just my thoughts and views. Get mad all you want, but when it comes right down to it, I'm right.

—*Bill "Superfoot" Wallace*

PART 1

❧

TRAINING
AND
FIGHTING

HOW SAFETY GEAR HAS CHANGED POINT KARATE

August 1990

There are many differences between the point fighting of my time and the point fighting of today. In the late '60s and early '70s, we didn't have safety equipment. There were no hand or foot pads, so we had to respect each other, and we had to have control. Even if we were mad enough to want to nail somebody, we still had to control our techniques because, if we hit a bone, we could break our knuckles just as easily as we could break the opponent's ribs.

Lack of safety gear also made it easier to pick out the guy who'd won by default. He'd go up to get the first-place trophy with his nose pushed over to the side of his face, two black eyes, maybe a gash on his forehead. He never touched anybody, but that's how he won—everybody else got disqualified for hitting him hard in the face.

So in a way, I'm glad for the advent of safety equipment. It helped answer the gripes about officiating, about what's a point and what's not a point, because during my time plenty of people griped about that, including me.

Safety gear allows a little contact to be made, and that's important. Back when we were fighting without the gear, the rules didn't allow any contact to the face. Usually I would go into a match and throw a roundhouse kick to the opponent's face and stop it about a foot away. Only one judge's flag

would go up, so I'd look at the other officials, shrug my shoulders and say, "All right, next time I'll just nail him." Of course, there was no way I was actually going to do that because I didn't want to get disqualified. But the next time I threw the kick, I'd maybe come a little closer. Maybe I'd only miss him by six inches. Suddenly the flags shoot up all around! So I used psychology. But did I score, or didn't I? The flags said I did, but we still don't know.

Around late 1972, hand and foot pads appeared. We started using them, and you could make contact to the face in the black belt divisions. You were allowed to touch lightly, which was good, because now you could prove that you really did score. In fact, in today's tournaments, where safety equipment is required, you almost have to make contact to score.

As a result, today's students are better at their techniques than we were, because they're allowed to make that little bit of contact. We were meaner and tougher back in the old days because our techniques were aimed at vital areas without pads, so we had to be tough. Today, the fighters train to hit; their techniques are designed to connect, thanks to the safety equipment.

The only question is, what do you score with today? In the 1960s and early '70s, the No. 1 point-getter was a reverse punch, one that was pulled just short of actual heavy contact. Except in Texas. In Texas, if you punched the guy in the body and dropped him, you got the point. But if you punched the guy in the face and dropped him, you either got a warning or got disqualified, depending on the amount of blood spilled. I liked to fight in Texas.

Since the advent of safety equipment, I'd say the top point-getters have become the ridgehand and the backfist. This is partly because there are ways to use the hand pads to sneakily extend your reach another six inches or so. Today, it's really become nothing more than a game of tag: If I touch you before you touch me, I win. That's another byproduct of the equipment.

I like the tournament rules today that require everybody to wear headgear. But if you wear headgear, I should be allowed to hit you in the head. In peewee football, they wear headgear, shoulder pads and all that football armor. Do they say you're not allowed to tackle? Of course not. They tackle. They learn how to take the shot, which is part of the game.

In most point karate today, I believe there is still no face contact allowed below the brown belt division, but you still have to wear headgear. I'm against that, simply because if I know the rules say you can't hit me in the face, I'm going to *lead* with my face. Then, if you hit me in the face, you get disqualified and, a few fights later, I get my trophy.

SO YOU WANT TO BE A FULL-CONTACT FIGHTER?

October 1990

Moving up from tournament sparring to full-contact karate is a step that requires a lot of preparation and also a lot of "unlearning." Speed, timing and distancing are the three major factors in point karate tournaments. They remain factors in full-contact karate, but now you have to add knockout power to the equation. Case in point: I remember hitting Joe Lewis with a reverse punch at a 1970 tournament that I thought would kill anybody. He just grabbed me, picked me up and dropped me on the floor. I'm only glad I found out about my reverse punch at a point tournament and not in the full-contact ring, where I would have been rocked with a counterpunch.

Next to power, you need conditioning. Most karate black belts have trained to hit, not to get hit. Well, you'll get hit in full-contact karate. Your opponent will be hitting you with power, and you have to train to take punishment. Point fighters don't have to take much punishment because (yeah, yeah, I know I've said this before) point fighting is a game of tag; if I hit you one second before you hit me, even though your hit is harder, I get the point. But in full-contact karate, a lot of times a fighter will let your first shot, like a jab, get in. The jab is not a strong technique, and it opens you up to a counter. You throw the jab, I lean back and don't care if it touches me, and I take your head off with a hook kick, a left hook or maybe even a side kick. Lewis was like that—you'd hit him, and your technique would just bounce off. He could take a good shot as well as give it.

On the other hand, consider another heavyweight full-contact fighter, Everett Eddy. He was massive, he hit hard and he was a very good fighter—a very good *point* fighter. The problem with Everett was his small neck, which meant (without going into too much anatomical detail) that he was more susceptible to a knockout than someone with a longer neck. I remember a boxer up in Ottawa knocked him out, then Ross Scott laid him flat in Las Vegas in 1977. Everett just couldn't take a shot.

Another major difference between point and full-contact fighters is their endurance. Point fighters have to go hard for only five to 10 seconds before the referee stops the action to call for points while they rest. You don't need endurance to be a good point fighter. Point tournament fighter Sammy Montgomery found out how difficult it is to make the transition to full-contact karate when he was knocked out in an early pro bout. But in full-contact karate, you can have all the power in the world, you can have all the conditioning in the world, but once you get tired, nothing happens, except *to* you. Endurance can be the deciding factor in a match.

The next thing to unlearn is your footwork. In point karate, you can stand there waving your arms after an exchange of techniques. I remember I used to turn my back on my opponent after I hit him with a good shot, knowing the referee would stop the match to call points. But fighting is continuous in full-contact karate, and you have to keep moving or be a sitting duck. A second big difference is that there are no out-of-bounds sections you can run to when you're in trouble. You're roped inside a square, and there's no place to go. If you get caught in a corner, good luck, because you can't turn, and you can't spin. You're stuck. So you have to learn to fight off the ropes, you have to learn distancing and you have to learn how to get out of the way.

Finally, forget the idea that what you'll be doing is full-contact *karate*. It's not really karate because you have gloved hands. You can't grab, so how can you throw anybody? And because the fighting is done so closely, it's very difficult to do any kind of jump-spinning kicks. If it were full-contact *karate*, they'd let you sweep, let you do the throwing techniques and let you do the jump-spinning kicks together with the close fighting. Now it's boxing with kicking, so kickboxing is an accurate name for the sport. (I'd rather it were called "boxkicking," however, because there's more boxing than kicking.)

There's a good reason for this: Once your hands are gloved, there are no better hand techniques in the world than boxing techniques—the jab, cross, hook, uppercut and the overhand. These are the techniques boxers use to fight, and these, rather than the backfist and the ridgehand, are the ones you'll be using in the full-contact ring.

In fact, you don't really need a background in point karate to succeed in kickboxing. There's a very good full-contact fighter named Bob Thurman who practiced karate, but he was never into point fighting. Kickboxing champion Jean-Yves Theriault is another. He's a yellow or purple belt in *jujutsu*, not in karate, but he's got very good boxing techniques and knows how to put punches and kicks together.

So I'm inclined to give the following advice: If you want to kickbox, don't do karate. Box first, then learn how to kick. That's where the sport's at right now.

EARLY LESSONS FROM FULL-CONTACT KARATE

November 1990

In last month's issue of *Black Belt* (October 1990), I discussed the difficulties in making the transition from point fighting to full-contact kickboxing. This month, I'd like to describe how I personally prepared for full-contact fighting and the lessons I learned during those early years.

Making that transition was like night and day. In point tournaments, I had developed a strategy around the rules they had for going out of bounds. Also, when the referee stopped the match to call for points, I took advantage of that time to recuperate. These were just two of the many things I couldn't do when I stepped into the ring for my first full-contact match in 1974. So I had to train drastically to prepare for my kickboxing career.

Building up endurance was my first priority. I ran two or three miles a day to increase my cardiovascular endurance, and I punched the heavy bag to build endurance in my upper body. Since I'm primarily a kicker, I

You learn to keep your eyes open, because it's not the punch you see that knocks you out, it's the one you don't see.

---

trained by kicking *a lot*; instead of just throwing five or six kicks to try to build speed, I would throw 30 or 40 side kicks nonstop so I could build endurance in my legs. After a while, I discovered I could do what I call "kicking rounds." A boxer will shadowbox the length of a full round nonstop, and I'd do the same thing, but I'd kick instead of punch.

When I sparred, I concentrated on timing and distancing. Now, when most people think of full-contact sparring, they think of two guys beating the heck out of each other. This approach doesn't help you; it just makes you sore the next day. You don't spar to develop power—that's what the heavy bag is for. When you spar, you should work on timing, distancing, movement, slipping punches, evading, countering, things like that—just like in point karate.

But in kickboxing, there's that added dimension of *contact*—you're getting hit, and getting hit hard. Because I wrestled and took judo before karate, I was used to getting hurt and getting drilled into the mat. But when I started training with boxers, I found I still hadn't gotten used to being hit. So I would train to get hit. I would stand there and let somebody hit me with hooks—not hard, of course, but just enough to get slapped, so you learn not to shut your eyes when you get hit. You learn to keep your eyes open, because it's not the punch you see that knocks you out, it's the one you don't see.

My first full-contact match was at the Los Angeles Sports Arena in September 1974 against Bernd Grothe of West Germany. It was billed as the World's Professional Karate Championships, and it was a preliminary bout for the world middleweight title. It was called full-contact karate, but it wasn't as brutal as it is now; at that time, it was more like "heavy, controlled contact."

We were wearing hand and foot pads, which were still new then, and we had to adjust to them. My kicks still worked because the padding was light on the feet, but I found out really quickly that, while a bare-knuckle backfist is very powerful, it doesn't have much effect when you're wearing a big glove. I hit Grothe full force with a padded backfist on the side of the face, and all it did was bounce off of him.

The same goes for the ridgehand. You can't really open the hand very much with the gloves they use in kickboxing, so how are you going to throw a ridgehand? These two basic point karate hand techniques, the backfist and ridgehand, simply didn't work in kickboxing, so, in about 1976, I started training with boxers. I had to unlearn the karate punching and learn how to throw a straight right hand from the chin. I had to learn how to throw an uppercut. Because I fought in a sideways karate stance, I concentrated on my left jab and left hook.

I'm primarily a distance fighter, and before I learned the boxing techniques, I relied on my judo background when someone got too close to me. In those days, from 1974 to 1978, throws were allowed, but in 1979 throws were eliminated because people didn't know how to throw properly. Guys kept falling on their heads or falling on their shoulders and hurting themselves. It began to look too sloppy, too much like wrestling, which was sad, because I really liked to throw opponents around. When they took the throws out in 1979, they moved the sport from karate toward boxing with kicking. That's why it is the way it is today.

UNLESS YOU'RE BILL WALLACE, DON'T KICK TO THE HEAD

June 1991

Many people ask me if, because I'm a good kicker, I would ever use a high kick to the head in a self-defense situation. Before I answer, consider the following three basic principles:

- **There are no referees in a street fight.**

If I throw a kick and my opponent grabs my leg, nobody will break us apart like they would in a tournament.

- **If I throw a high kick, chances are I'll be very close to my opponent, and I run the risk of jamming myself.**

In most street fights or bar fights, the fighters are within two or three feet of each other. People don't stand across the bar, stare at each other and say, "Come on dude, let's fight." Rather, they stand right in front of each other, and one guy tries to lay the other guy out.

- **Depending on where I fight—in a bar, on the street, in an alley or wherever—there will be an awfully good chance of slipping when I go to throw the kick.**

You never know how much beer or water is on the ground. When I fight on a mat or in a ring, I know how slippery it is because I get the chance to try it out first. But there are guys who get attacked on the street and try to do a spinning back kick. They're going to land on their faces, and there won't be any officials saying, "Stop, stop. Let him up."

If you kick to the head, you need the flexibility, strength and balance to get that leg up there and put your foot exactly where you want it. I've been stretching consistently for a long time, so it's easy for me to kick somebody in the head without warming up. It's difficult for somebody who's been practicing karate for only two or three years to throw a high kick without stretching, and it's even more difficult if you're wearing jeans or tight pants. Also, keep in mind that you'll probably be wearing shoes in a street fight, and even light shoes can affect your balance.

I'm not saying completely avoid high kicks in a self-defense situation. If there were two or more assailants, I might hit one guy upside the head with a roundhouse or a hook kick and drop him really fast. The other guys would hopefully think, "Whoa, what was that? Maybe we picked on the wrong guy."

But, generally, head kicks are not as effective as kicks to the attacker's body or legs. Rather than use high kicks in a self-defense situation, kick the assailant in the knee. Make him bend over, *then* kick him in the head.

Or, better yet, just turn around and take off.

A WORLD OF HURT

April 1992

Most martial artists have done some type of damage to themselves while training or competing, from the top of their heads all the way down to their toes. I'm no exception. I get hurt just like everybody else.

In karate training, I find that the most frequent injuries are to the toes, because when you throw kicks, you throw them barefooted. Even though you might have padding on your feet, you still mangle the toes a little bit by hitting elbows or knees. Toes are inevitably going to get jammed or dislocated, and sometimes even broken. It happens all the time. Bruising is also common. When you throw hard techniques, you're going to bruise. This happens mostly to your arms and legs.

These injuries heal, but sometimes in the course of training, you'll do something that doesn't heal quickly. Ligaments, for example, take a very long time to heal, and they never really heal completely. Most people know that I kick with my left leg. I tore the medial collateral ligament in my right knee during a judo training session in 1966. Doctors told me there was a 50 percent chance I'd be able to use the leg again.

The harder I worked, the more it hurt, but I started playing judo again anyway until 1971, when I tore my knee up for the second time. I still train a little bit in judo, but I have to wear a heavy knee brace. I never kick with my right leg, because if I throw a kick with that leg and I don't make contact, the knee comes out of joint and my leg flies across the room.

Any time you have contact, you're going to have bruises and you're going to get cut. The sharp bones above the eyes will eventually tear your skin if you get hit in that area all the time. And you're going to get a bloody nose if your nose gets hit enough. Don't worry about these little things, though, because there are far worse injuries.

The worst injury I ever had was a deviated septum. The septum is the little bridge in your nose that separates the nostrils. I was working out with this guy, just going nice and easy. I had him in the corner, working on some body shots, when all of a sudden he lifted up and the top of his head hit me square in the nose. My nose didn't bleed—it gushed. It took me 15 minutes to stop the bleeding. When I got home, it didn't hurt much, but it was throbbing. My nose looked straight, so I knew it wasn't broken, but when I tilted my head back, I could see that the septum was crooked and mangled. It still is today.

The nose is 99 percent cartilage. If you hit it hard enough, you'll crush or twist that cartilage. And cartilage doesn't grow back straight. When it heals, it will still be mangled, or "deviated." That's why most boxers, kickboxers, Thai boxers and wrestlers have flat noses to some degree.

Your hands also get hurt fairly often. When you hit a heavy bag, you have to put wraps or gloves on your hands to protect them. But sometimes, if you punch hard enough, your wrist will twist or you'll hit the knuckles wrong, causing injury.

The injury to my knee was serious enough that it forced me to stop participating in sports that I enjoyed, but I made some adjustments to my life and moved on. When I was in Africa last summer, I had another rather serious problem. I was teaching some actors how to box for an upcoming movie, and I think I pulled my left hip out of joint. I was showing them how to dance around like Muhammad Ali and, as I was bouncing, I felt my hip pop out. That happened three times. The first couple of times, it just felt funny. The third time, it hurt, but it went right back into place, and I thought nothing of it.

The day after I got back to the United States, I got up and couldn't take a step; I couldn't bend cver to touch my knees, let alone my toes. I had to hobble around everywhere. The muscle that runs through the hip joint up to the rib cage was inflamed and swollen, and I couldn't straighten it. It took a month and a half of rest before I could do any stretching, let alone throw a kick. I had to let it heal. If I had tried to stretch it, I would have hurt the muscle even more.

When you strain muscles, ligaments or tendons, you have to let them rest—and not just for a day or two. Your body is a wonderful machine, but you have to relax and let time take its course. I still have a little pain left over from that strain, but I can kick and I can walk just fine. If you're hurt, all I can say is let your body repair itself. That's the secret to overcoming martial arts injuries.

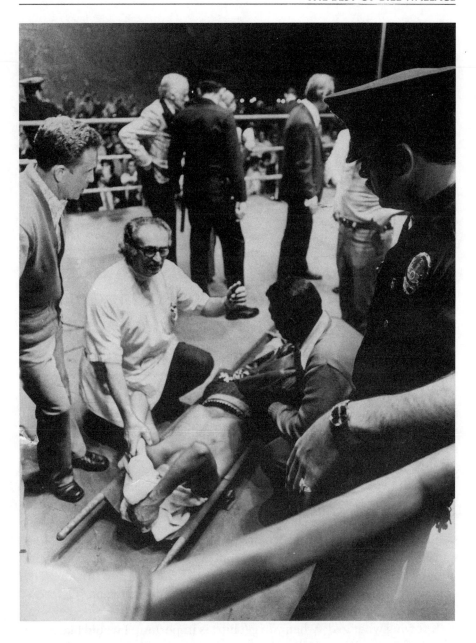

IT'S YOUR BODY—TREAT IT WELL

May 1992

In last month's issue of *Black Belt* (April 1992), I wrote about the importance of rest when treating martial arts injuries. A rested and relaxed muscle is a faster-healing muscle because you have more blood flowing through the fibers. That's just one general tip. There are actually lots of specific things you can do to help your injuries.

When you jam a finger, which all of us do sooner or later, straighten it out and immobilize it. Put a splint on it so it can heal. I'm a big believer in braces and wraps. If you immobilize an injured joint, you can keep training with the parts of your body that aren't hurt.

I would like to see schools that teach sports like karate, judo, boxing and wrestling instruct their students in the treatment of common injuries.

If you twist your ankle, elevate the foot and put ice on it. By elevating the appendage, you allow less blood to travel to the foot. The ice will restrict the blood flow in the arteries and capillaries and keep the foot from swelling. If you're wearing shoes, don't take them off, because the foot will swell up like a balloon.

If you hurt your knee, keep it straight if possible. The muscles will relax easier if the leg is straight owing to the anatomical structure of the body.

Cuts should always be elevated above the heart. Sometimes I see people stand up quickly after getting a bloody nose. Actually, all you have to do is squeeze your nose and hold it closed for about a minute. That will keep it from bleeding. Don't swallow that stuff, because it's hard to breathe. The same goes for cuts over the eyes. Don't pull the cut apart and go, "Wow, look at that!" Rather, simply pinch the cut closed.

Knowing what to do when you get hurt is important. I would like to see schools that teach sports like karate, judo, boxing and wrestling instruct their students in the treatment of common injuries. If you twist your wrist, ankle or knee, or if you get bruised, there are things you can do. Some people will say, "You have to go see a doctor." Well, that's true. But there are some things that you can do at the time of the injury.

The main thing is, take care of your body after it gets injured. Everybody tries to take care of it *before* an injury: They use tape on their fingers, wear kneepads, etc. But you only get one body. Take care of it. If you keep injuring that same part of the body, it's only going to get worse. Sometimes a football player gets injured, and he says, "I'll be back in three weeks." Sure, he's back in three weeks, but he's not totally fit, and it's really easy for him to re-injure that part of his body. It happens all the time.

If you've had an injury, and you kept hurting it repeatedly for six months, taking several months off isn't going to help. Now your body is used to having a stretched ligament or muscle. It's going to take longer to get the muscles back where they're supposed to be than it took to injure them in the first place.

Remember, you can train without working the injured part of your body. If I hurt my knee, that doesn't mean I can't work the heavy bag with my punches or shadowbox. If I hurt my right hand, I can still practice with the left jab and the left hook or work on my kicks. There's always ways of getting around an injury. That's what I've had to do with my right leg throughout my career.

So protect yourself. Learn to take care of your body. There are hundreds of books on the subject. Take a course or two in first aid or sports medicine. It's the only body you've got, and you've got to treat it well.

DO YOU WANT TO DANCE?

October 1992

A lthough most people remember me from my full-contact and point karate fighting in the late '60s, I also competed in *kata*. I trained with Glen Keeney, who was a very good kata competitor. Back then, whenever Keeney entered a kata division, I said, "Well, heck, so will I." I was not a great kata competitor, but I placed second or third a couple of times. Some people said that I had good technique (and I agree), but my heart was not in forms. I liked punching and kicking toward people, not at the air.

Traditional Japanese karate instructors probably think, "OK, fight me like that. Come on. Do a back flip. As soon as you land, I'm going to take your face off."

A lot of the techniques used in kata would be useless in an actual fighting situation. Kata competition today is basically a beauty contest to determine who dresses the nicest and can do the most somersaults or back flips. It's not really martial arts anymore. It is, like Jhoon Rhee has said, "martial ballet." It's a dance. The kata competitors come out and do gymnastics and maybe throw some punches and kicks. People like to see that, but it has nothing to do with martial arts.

I was in the Cayman Islands recently, and some kids asked me if I could do back flips like they had seen in martial arts movies. I said, "No. Every time I try to do a back flip, I land flat on my face."

I notice that they don't even call it kata these days. They call it "forms competition." If they are going to allow these unrealistic kata at tournaments, they should at least have separate divisions for traditional forms and creative forms. Some people might be able to do an absolutely fantastic traditional kata, but the judges won't give them a decent score because there is another guy who is dancing all around the floor.

Granted, people want to see all the fancy gymnastics, but it's not kata anymore. When old, traditional Japanese karate instructors look at that stuff, they just kind of giggle. They probably think, "OK, fight me like that. Come on. Do a back flip. As soon as you land, I'm going to take your face off."

The forms you see today at tournaments don't have very much to do with actual fighting, which is why very few kata competitors perform very successfully in sparring competitions. George Chung did very fine forms—he was the national champion for several years in the 1980s—but he didn't fight that much. Charlie Lee was another national forms champion, but I don't think he ever fought. Not that these guys *can't* fight; they might be very good fighters. But in a real fight, you have to keep your hands in front of your face to protect yourself, and you can't pull the hand back to throw that reverse punch you learned in a form. It takes too long. You sacrifice something in the technique.

It all boils down to this: Are you going to make the techniques effective, or do you want them to be pretty? I like effective much better.

MY FAVORITE HAND TECHNIQUES

July 1993

I have two favorite hand techniques. For karate tournaments, my favorite hand technique is the backfist, and during my career in full-contact karate, I found the left hook very effective.

I started using a backfist because I needed a technique that would help set up my kicks. It also served as a defensive move. If someone charged me and I couldn't get my leg up in time, I could just stick the backfist right in his face and hopefully score.

Although no one really influenced my backfist, I have to thank Glenn Keeney of Anderson, Indiana, for helping me the most with it. We sparred a lot, and it was difficult for me to score on him with my kicks because he was so familiar with my moves, so I used the backfist to set up different maneuvers. I didn't practice it that much, though. Once I got the snap of the elbow down, there was nothing else to work on. The two most important things were timing and distance. I wanted to be certain I got my opponent before he got too close to me.

The backfist was great for tournament sparring because it was fairly quick. I fought with my left hand down, making it hard for my opponent to see it. I could snap it out real quick for a backfist.

Although I enjoyed success with the backfist at karate tournaments, I had a problem with it when I began my professional full-contact karate career. In tournament karate, when you strike with the first two knuckles of your fist, you have good power and good penetration. On the other hand, the same tournament techniques become null and void when you wore eight- or 10-ounce boxing gloves; when you wear gloves, certain punches might slow an opponent down, but they won't stop him. For these strikes to be effective, they have to be modified so they can be used with power—you need to use your hips and shoulders, not just your arms, which is difficult to learn. If you watch karate practitioners shadowbox, they look silly because they are stiff from the waist up. They are not used to using shoulder power. A boxer, on the other hand, is always moving his hips and shoulders to build up torque.

Therefore, to make my backfist effective for full-contact karate, I had to modify it. In 1976, I started working with Joe Lewis and Joey Hadley, a boxer from Memphis. They showed me how to move and how to spar using a jab. Sometimes I would even tie my right hand behind my back and jab with my left arm so I could focus on the timing and distance. In kickboxing, you are trying to take a guy's head off or score with a good, solid technique. But when you throw a backfist in tournament sparring, you snap it out really fast and just try to get a point. So I had to change my backfist and throw it straight into my opponent, like a half-jab. This was a simple transition because it was a matter of survival; it was either change the backfist or get beat up. As it turned out, I was able to keep everybody off of me with the modified backfist.

My other favorite hand technique is the left hook, and I found out in high school that I had a natural one. I got in a fight with someone much bigger than I, and without thinking, I hit him with a left hook and dropped him. As he went down, I said, "Whoa."

Although I had a natural left hook, Lewis was the first one who taught me how to use it effectively. He and Bevo Covington refined it and made it quicker by shortening it. I worked on the punch from my side stance, because I didn't want to change my kicking technique by changing to a traditional boxing stance.

When I fought Gary Eatons in Los Angeles in 1976, I dropped him with a short left hook to the chin 15 seconds into the match, and I thought to myself, "I guess I've learned how to throw a left hook."

My two hand techniques were not the best in the world, but they worked for me. The key to my suc-cess was modification. I did not throw my left hook like a lot of people did. When I practiced the punch against a heavy bag, I did it from the hips, and I didn't turn my hand over like a boxer would. I didn't hit with the knuckles, I hit with the whole fist area.

Each person has to do what feels right. A student needs to take four or five techniques that he feels comfortable with and modify them so they work effectively. If he works with them for a long time, he'll become more comfortable with them and they'll become instinctive.

Photo by Rick Hustead

MARTIAL ARTS MYSTERIES: FACT OR FICTION

February 1994

Most people who want to practice the martial arts want to do so for the self-defense benefits. They want to learn a nice, quick, mystical way to defeat the enemy without having to sweat much or get hit. They want to learn self-defense techniques that will work against anybody. They want to learn in two days a technique that will allow them to beat up someone who has trained in the martial arts for 35 years.

So they sign up for a martial arts class. They learn the reverse punch and throw hundreds of them during their first night of training. Their instructor tells them how devastating the technique is: "If you use this in a self-defense situation, it will cause so much trauma and shock that your attacker will never bother you again."

After four or five weeks of training, they begin to spar with other students. They throw their best reverse punch and hit their opponents in the ribs, but their opponents just back up and say, "Good shot." They begin to worry that it will be difficult to protect themselves, so their instructors come up with excuses: The technique didn't have good focus, it missed a vital point or it did not possess enough *chi* energy. But who are they kidding?

I don't believe in martial arts mysticism. I don't believe any person can knock out another person with a secret nerve strike or use a delayed-effect "death touch" or some mystical application of chi energy. Martial arts techniques are 100 percent physical and scientific.

Some techniques are designed to hit a particular area for maximum effect. Others are designed to cause damage, no matter where they hit. The effect might not become immediately apparent—a person can get hit in a specific area and get bruised, and after a while the injury might get worse—but that's not the same as a death touch that takes effect six months later.

I also don't believe in miracle touches, where a guy hits a person and, three seconds later, the victim drops to the floor. If anything like that happens, it can be explained medically; if someone hits the carotid artery on your neck, for example, you will fall down after a few seconds, simply because the blood supply to your brain was cut off. It's like the judo chop—everybody used to think it was devastating and mysterious until someone explained it medically.

These days we hear a lot about martial artists who demonstrate how to knock people out with a secret nerve strike. The technique usually works because the instructor knocks the living piss out of the volunteer when he performs it. Even if the nerve strike doesn't knock him out, the punch itself is powerful enough to do it. Some people demonstrate knockout techniques by hitting a guy hard in the forehead and grabbing the back of his neck at the same time. This way he receives a multiple shock.

If these nerve strikes really worked, professional boxers would use them. They get paid millions to fight. If they could knock out an opponent by hitting him with the thumb of a boxing glove, they certainly would. You can't argue that gloves prevent boxers from using nerve strikes, because if people can get penetration with a bare thumb in a clinch, they should also be able to do so with the thumb of a gloved hand.

I don't believe any person can knock out another person with a secret nerve strike or use a delayed-effect "death touch" or some mystical application of chi energy.

I don't believe people who claim to use their chi energy to defeat opponents. Chi is supposed to elevate your mind over your body (or your mind over your opponent's body, as the case may be). But something has to travel through the air to have an effect. I haven't found anybody yet who could beat another person by just thinking or talking. People can build up their chi to fight better, but they can't use chi to directly attack an opponent. The problem is that we believe our instructors when they say, "My chi defeated you." Even though it isn't logical, students want to believe it because they want to learn mystical, less-strenuous methods of self-defense.

I am 100 percent into the physical aspects of martial arts. I like sparring, training and working on techniques. The only part of my training that might be considered mystical is the mental portion of the workout: I try to make everything perfect, even though I know it never will be.

MARTIAL ARTISTS ARE MERELY MORTALS

July 1994

Every time a martial artist is murdered or injured, the media emphasizes the person's martial arts training, as if they expect martial artists to be immune from injury. Some martial artists add to this false impression because they also think they're invincible; they practice their punches and kicks and think they will automatically be able to use their training against any attack.

The problem with this is that these martial artists assume their opponents will confront them head-on, or that they'll have some sort of warning before an attack from the rear. Martial artists know how to defend themselves in certain situations, but if they have no warning, they're almost as vulnerable as everyone else. If someone attacks from the back and catches them off-guard, their first reaction will be shock rather than to punch or block. And nobody can stop that initial reaction.

What members of the media have to understand is that martial artists are human beings. If I can't breathe, I die just like everyone else. If someone sticks a knife in my back, I can bleed to death. If you point a gun at me and pull the trigger, it's awfully hard to defend against bullets. But you see all kinds of articles in martial arts magazines in which they talk about this *chi* energy that allows you to feel somebody's presence. I think that's a bunch of bull. You might have internal alarms that make you suspect something is going to happen, but that's just instinct, and you don't need years of martial arts training for that.

> *Martial artists know how to defend themselves in certain situations, but if they have no warning, they're almost as vulnerable as everyone else.*

Granted, self-defense training does heighten the senses, so martial artists will have some advantages over the general public when faced with a life-or-death situation. Their reflexes should be a little quicker and their movements a little more precise. But nobody can close his eyes and catch an opponent's fist in midpunch. That only happens in the movies, and it's garbage.

The media has the perception that martial artists are invincible, because the media believes what it sees in the movies. They believe that Jean-Claude Van Damme can jump in the air and kick eight people in the head before landing. They believe that Steven Seagal can wipe out 31 professional terrorists, like he did in *Under Siege*. (If he can really do that, you wonder why he has bodyguards.) Even if martial artists have perfected every skill, every technique, every move, they will be just as vulnerable as anyone else if they panic or if their emotions get in the way of their training.

I was at the Battle of Atlanta last year, and during the team fighting competition, Hakeem Alston of Washington fought Mike Schmidt of Florida. Schmidt took Alston down and hit him without much force to the face. Alston got up, and he was mad as hell. As soon as the match was over, he took a Sunday-haymaker swing at Schmidt, who was just standing there, and *missed*. Maybe he was upset, nervous, scared, mad or whatever, but he'd never been in that situation before.

Fear and panic keep you from being able to defend yourself in a real situation. When you panic, you get tired. And when you get tired, you get frustrated, and you don't use your mind. Most people's first reaction to an attack is to panic or freeze up, and most self-defense classes don't teach you how to overcome that fear. But if you study martial arts, you can keep your cool, and you should be able to defend yourself in a real attack.

IT'S OK TO FIGHT DIRTY

January 1995

A lot of traditional martial artists don't believe in dirty fighting of any kind. These individuals would never consider biting an opponent or pulling his hair. But I think a person should use whatever he can in the street to defend himself, even if he is a trained martial artist. Nothing is too dirty.

If somebody comes up and picks a fight with me, and his crotch is vulnerable to attack, I'm going to take that shot because it's a great target. Discipline and restraint are wonderful if you're out someplace and a casual argument ensues. But you're not going to be able to reason with some guy with a knife who wants to take your money. Turning the other cheek might have worked in the past, when people walked around with sticks and stones or bows and arrows. But now guys are walking around with guns, and if they don't get your money, they'll take your rings and your fingers with them.

I think a person should use whatever he can in the street to defend himself, even if he is a trained martial artist.

Some people say you should use only the amount of force needed to end an altercation, and anything more is overkill. But I don't think there is such a thing as overkill. If someone is threatening you, how do you know he doesn't have a weapon? You have to be prepared for anything. You can't go around attacking everyone who comes near you, but if somebody comes up and says, "I'm going to give you a beating," what are you going to do? Walk away from him?

A karate tournament has rules, and everyone abides by those rules. The person you're sparring at the tournament doesn't have a gun or a knife in his pocket. He doesn't have three friends hiding behind the referee, waiting to jump you when your back is turned. There are rules at tournaments to keep people from getting hurt. Even the street challenges they had in the old days had certain rules of conduct, and you had the advantage of knowing who you were fighting. If you challenged me, we'd go out and fight at a designated time. In the Philippines, they still have rumbles like these, in which two gangs meet at a neutral area and fight. The gang leaders meet beforehand to decide what weapons will be allowed—switchblades, knives, sticks, guns—and then they go at it.

But when you're walking down the street and some guy confronts you and says, "I want your money," you don't know whether he's alone or whether there are three other guys around the corner. You don't know if he's got a gun or a knife in his possession. All you know is that he wants to do you harm. If you see a target—whether it's his knee, throat, groin or eyes—you should hit it, because you might never have that chance again. If you don't take advantage of your opponent's mistakes, it could cost you your life.

The martial arts give you an aura that others respect. They teach restraint and bestow confidence. If a drunk comes up to you and starts talking trash, that's the time to use proper restraint. But if the guy has a knife, a gun or a club and is out for blood, you have to have the confidence to hit him and hit him hard, and make sure he doesn't get back up.

SUPERFOOT'S HOME WORKOUT

November 1996

I do a lot of my workouts at home. To me, it is much more relaxing than working out at a gym. Plus, with all the traveling I do, I don't always have the time or means to get to a gym. I have to be able to workout quickly and use whatever is available, so I figured out a very simple yet effective way to train at home or in a hotel room when I travel.

The first thing I do is warm up nice and easy, moving my hips, arms, elbows and shoulders. Some people take too long to warm up. This is just a short session to stretch the muscles and get the blood flowing.

After warming up, I start my workout with three sets of 30 push-ups, resting for one minute between each set. I do push-ups on my knuckles, because that also works my forearms along with the triceps and chest. Sometimes I keep my hands close together, and other times I keep them far apart, but I try to always keep my back perfectly straight and touch my chest to the floor. I keep my fists parallel to my body, simulating a straight punch. In that way, I get the muscle memory of the punch.

After completing three sets of push-ups, I do three sets of 30 dips between two chairs. I put my hands on one chair, palms away from me, and my feet on the other chair. This drill works my triceps and my lats.

After the dips, it's time for pull-ups. Virtually every bathroom has a door, which I open and place a folded towel tightly underneath. This way it won't break or move when I hang on it. I drape a towel over the top of the door to protect my hands, grab the top of the door, bend my knees and pull myself to the top of the door or until my head touches the ceiling. I perform three sets of 15 pull-ups. The neat part about pull-ups is that you're lifting your own weight, which really isolates the chest and biceps. And, by gripping the door, you're also working your forearms, which usually don't get exercised very much. Most guys' forearms aren't very big. They also work my quadriceps and abdominal muscles, because I push myself away from the door with my knees as I pull myself up.

After pull-ups, I put my feet under the bed and do three sets of sit-ups, placing my hands on my stomach rather than behind my neck to avoid straining my back. I then lay flat on the floor and perform three sets of 30 neck rotations.

Now that I'm nice and tired, I relax a little and stretch. Most people take way too long to stretch out. If you're sore after stretching, you know you took too long. I take five or 10 minutes to stretch. I move my legs out to a certain position, hold it for 30 or 40 seconds, then move them a little farther apart and hold that stretch for another 30 to 40 seconds. This way, the muscles learn to relax in that position. It also gives the muscles in my upper body a chance to relax.

Because you're not taking the muscles to full exhaustion, you can perform this group of exercises every day. I've got it down to where it takes me about 15 minutes to perform all of the exercises I've mentioned. You can add or subtract repetitions or add sets if you wish. I do three sets of each exercise, but if you're feeling really good, you might want to do five or more. Or you could do three sets of 50 repetitions. The important thing is that you're working the muscles, keeping them toned, and not letting them atrophy.

If you want to incorporate some martial arts into the workout, you can always stand up, hold onto a chair and execute slow kicks. After I stretch, I'll hold onto a chair and do maybe 50 slow roundhouse kicks, holding my knee as high as I can. Then I execute another 50 side kicks. These don't have to be high, but the movement should be absolutely correct. Bring the knee up and stick the leg out straight, then bring it back. Then I'll do some slow hook kicks. These really build the quadriceps. Because this drill takes time, it builds your cardiovascular endurance, making your heart work a little bit.

This workout is perfect for my body because I'm not trying to build muscle bulk. It maintains my strength, and because it has high repetitions, it also helps my speed, flexibility and muscle memory—even when I travel.

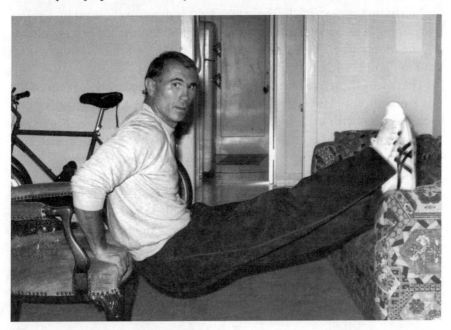

WEIGHT TRAINING FOR THE MARTIAL ARTS

February 1997

People generally have one of two goals when they lift weights: They either want to build muscle bulk, or they want to improve muscle speed. The general theory is, use small amounts of weight and perform many repetitions to build muscle speed and endurance, and use larger amounts of weight and fewer repetitions to build muscle bulk and strength.

You should isolate different muscle groups and work them separately when training with weights. Every time you move a muscle, an antagonistic muscle is working against the movement. These are known as adductor and abductor muscles, and they draw body parts toward and away from the body, respectively.

Most martial artists are better off lifting lighter weights with more repetitions.

Make sure to fully extend the muscles you're working, stretching them out completely before making a full contraction. You should work each muscle group only about twice a week, allowing each muscle group to rest and recover.

Martial artists, especially those who fight competitively, want to develop both strength and speed when they lift weights. But the more weight they lift, the more muscle bulk they build, which creates additional weight they have to control when executing a punch or kick.

That's why most martial artists are better off lifting lighter weights with more repetitions. They could, for example, perform five to seven sets of each exercise, with each set consisting of 12 to 15 repetitions. There are many programs and exercises that build muscle strength and speed, and each individual must discover what method works best for him.

Martial artists who are good kickers tend to have legs that aren't very muscular, and they can kick faster than others because they don't have as much weight to lift. Martial artists with slender legs don't have to lean their bodies back to prepare to execute the kick; they can just deliver it from an upright position, much like a boxer throwing a jab.

Martial artists can, however, build kicking speed by using leg weights when they train. In the United States, most of the leg weights are 2 to 3 ounces. In Europe, however, they have leg weights that are 6 to 8 ounces, which make a big difference when attempting a kick. After training with leg weights, you'll be amazed at how light and quick your legs feel without them.

I'm 51, and I still enjoy lifting weights. My current routine is not much different from what it was when I competed as a kickboxer and tournament fighter. When I was fighting, however, I would go to the gym *after* competing, as well as before. I primarily do bench presses, dips, military presses, tricep extensions and dumbbell curls. I limit myself to three sets of each exercise, whereas bodybuilders push their muscles to exhaustion, spending four to six hours a day in the gym. I just want to maintain and tone the muscles I already have rather than build size. Weight training also gives me a chance to work off those extra calories.

KNOCKOUT KICKS

June 1998

Because I had a bad knee during my kickboxing career, I used only three kicks: the side kick, the roundhouse kick and the front-leg hook kick. The hook kick and side kick were my main power shots, as they are for many martial artists. They could work on their own and get the job done.

Whenever I executed a side kick, it was a driving shot to the body. In competition, I scored several knockouts with it. Because nearly all martial artists know how to execute the side kick, I won't discuss it any further.

The roundhouse kick with the front leg, however, is a different story, because many don't know how to use it effectively. Generally, the kick doesn't have a lot of power—it's just very fast. Much like a boxer's jab, it stings a little bit. During all the years I kickboxed, I knocked out only one person with the technique, owing more to the speed of the kick than its power.

On the other hand, if you want power, the rear-leg roundhouse kick is a good technique to use. The spinning back kick and the spinning hook kick are also powerful. You can use fast kicks to create openings for other, more powerful techniques. In my competition days, I often used a roundhouse kick to the stomach to set people up. This kick would make the opponent drop his elbows, allowing me to blast his head.

Even though a stomach-level roundhouse doesn't initially hurt, after a while it begins to sting. Oftentimes, this little roundhouse kick to the stomach becomes embarrassing because the opponent's stomach area starts to turn red and he begins to think about the impact. This can set him up for another kick, which could be devastating. I've never knocked the wind out of anybody with a roundhouse kick to the stomach, but it makes a nice, loud pop, and it scores points. And if the fight goes the distance, these points can help a person win.

When I competed, I was fortunate to have a very effective front-leg hook kick. Even though it was not quite as powerful as the side kick, I had three or four knockouts with it when I was able to catch my opponent as he was coming at me.

To increase the power of the hook kick, I would just throw it out and let it snap through. When most people throw this kick, they just swing it back without the whipping motion, but I used to throw mine like a whip for maximum effectiveness. For example, I might throw a hook kick to your face, but rather than aiming right at your face, I would aim it a foot and a half to two feet to the left of your face and let the whipping motion take care of itself. Also, I always tried to hit my target with the heel or flat part of the foot. I also used the hook kick to distract the opponent. When I threw it at him, he had to block it because he knew it was one of my knockout shots. As soon as he did this, another target became available.

When talking about effective knockout kicks, very few people mention torque—the twisting force behind the kick that makes it powerful. When you throw a roundhouse with the rear leg, you twist your body as you bring the leg around, and it's this torque that creates knockout power.

These days, many people are wondering if they should avoid going for a knockout kick aimed at their opponent's head. Instead, they say it's better to go for the leg or the body. I disagree. Head kicks are fine, as long as they're done correctly and at the right time. They've scored plenty of knockouts in the ring and will continue to do so.

EFFECTIVE KICKS

July 1998

This column is the conclusion of a two-part series that discusses kicks and their use in competition and self-defense. Part one appeared in the June 1998 issue.

I've always considered the side kick to be a power shot. Even though it's a snappy kick in many ways, you should concentrate on driving it into the target, which is usually your opponent's body.

Some martial artists believe the side kick can be used to strike their opponent in the face, but I seldom threw one to the head unless my opponent was bent over. I preferred to throw the kick to his body to get him to lower his arms, then I'd throw something to the head. I also used the side kick as a counterattack because I usually had a sideways fighting stance. When my opponent came in with his hands up to throw a punch, I would drop him with a side kick to the body, using my heel or the side of my foot to make contact.

If you watch a point-karate tournament, it's easy to spot the guy who uses a lot of front kicks, because he's the one limping; when you throw a front kick, the toes often hit an elbow, a knee, a hip or something else.

The front kick can also be a powerful technique, but be careful. If you watch a point-karate tournament, it's easy to spot the guy who uses a lot of front kicks, because he's the one limping; when you throw a front kick, the toes often hit an elbow, a knee, a hip or something else. The average *muay Thai* fighter likes to use front kicks because his opponents—also Thai boxers—tend to keep their elbows out of the way. This leaves the path to the abdomen wide open for the kick.

As for spinning kicks, they should be used only against a stunned or bewildered opponent. There are a lot of martial artists—Korean stylists, for example—who are very effective with the spinning back kick. A good prac-

titioner can execute it with speed and power because of the reverse torque in the body. On the negative side, the kick is difficult to control, especially when thrown to your opponent's head. They're also easily countered in a kickboxing match because, if you miss your target, you can't easily stop the kick and you leave yourself open.

Another point to consider: Many martial artists say that you should never turn your back on your opponent in a kickboxing match or no-holds-barred fight. I agree with this. When you do a spinning back kick in a kickboxing match, your back is turned only for a split second, but your opponent still has the opportunity to pound you in the back of the head if

STREET FIGHTING IS DIFFERENT FROM COMPETITION

September 1998

Street fighting is a whole different ballgame than competitive fighting. Many moves and strategies that are effective in competition can actually get you into deep trouble if you try them in the street. Two good hand techniques, like the jab and hook, and two good kicks, like the side and front kick, are all you need to be effective at street self-defense.

On the street, throws and chokes are hard to execute. When you get attacked in real life, you never know whether two or three other guys are in the vicinity. You don't want to take your opponent down and wrestle around with him, hoping to catch him with a choke or armbar. Your opponent's buddies could be waiting for you to go to the ground so they can beat the pulp out of you with kicks and punches. You will not know whether nails, glass or other sharp objects are on the ground before you take your opponent down. I don't know about you, but I don't want to roll around on that stuff. You might be wearing a suit or other nice clothes, and at the very least you're going to get bruised and scraped. Also, your adversary might be an excellent wrestler. It has always been my view that it's best to get in and out as quickly as you can.

One thing I've always told myself is, if someone comes at me with a knife, he might cut me, but I'm going to blast him with a side kick as hard as I can possibly throw it, and whatever is in the way is going to get hurt.

How can you end a street fight in your favor? A street fight begins and ends quickly if you hit your opponent with something he can't see or react to, like a fast jab to the face or a side kick to the body. You can do a lot of damage if you hit someone in the stomach with a good, hard side kick—especially if you're wearing shoes. If you take that same side kick and direct it toward your opponent's knee, you can do even more damage. One thing I've always told myself is, if someone comes at me with a knife, he might cut me, but I'm going to blast him with a side kick as hard as I can possibly throw it, and whatever is in the way is going to get hurt.

The jab can also quickly end a potentially disastrous confrontation. For example, let's say you are faced with three attackers. If you stick one of the guys in the nose with a nice, stiff jab, his nose will probably start bleeding and he'll be momentarily stunned. Seeing their friend all bloody might give the remaining attackers pause, and the fight could end right there, or it could give you time to run away.

One of the problems I have with traditional self-defense training is the emphasis on executing a "finishing technique." If you hit someone with a good punch or kick, why should you stick around and finish him off? I have never quite understood the logic behind that strategy. I've never been a believer in finishing a fight. Getting out of danger as quickly as possible is the best technique of all.

PROS AND CONS OF TAE-BO AEROBICS
August 1999

I am happy to see good people excel in the martial arts—for example, Southern California-based Tae-Bo guru Billy Blanks. He couples great athletic ability with a great idea, and he has been able to cash in on it. However, in addition to some praise, I would like to offer some constructive criticism.

Strengths

Tae-Bo is an energetic exercise done to music, and Blanks and his instructors give it an infusion of energy that rubs off onto the students. Through Tae-Bo, they build their rhythm, stamina, strength and endurance. Blanks has created a phenomenal training exercise, and everyone involved has done an excellent job marketing it.

I've worked out with Blanks several times, and he's an excellent fighter. We had a good time sparring together. Blanks' associates are also excellent fighters, and that expertise is imparted to their students. Blanks' success has blazed the way for others to do similar things. He's helped fledgling schools that can now teach cardio-karate and cardio-kickboxing to stay in business. Many of these schools now have more fitness people than karate people. Also, many Tae-Bo students may very well let their curiosity get the best of them and enroll in traditional karate classes.

Billy Blanks has created a phenomenal training exercise, and everyone involved has done an excellent job marketing it.

Weaknesses

As much as I like what Blanks has done, there are some problems with his program. The instructors should consider having their students stretch prior to working out to prevent hyperextension of their elbows and knees. There have been reports of Blanks getting into legal trouble because students have injured themselves during class.

Also, students should be taught how to do the techniques correctly. For example, throwing a kick out and just letting the leg drop instead of snapping it back is bad for the joints, cartilage and ligaments. Blanks should take a few minutes before the workout to show his students how to properly execute the hand and foot techniques. The students would probably enjoy learning the meaning behind the kicks and punches they're throwing.

In his infomercials, some of Blanks' female students claim their training makes them feel safer on the street. This is misleading. Tae-Bo students are only throwing punches and kicks to music; they're not learning self-defense. They have no idea what the techniques are for.

Also, with the phenomenal success of his tapes and schools, I don't understand why Blanks feels a need to claim he is a seven-time world martial arts champion. That gets back to the question of illegitimate world-championship titles, which I've discussed in previous columns. He did win the Battle of Atlanta one year when it was called a world championship. Why can't he just say "world champion"? A few years ago, when I worked out with Blanks, he was a four-time world champion. He hasn't fought at all since then, so how could he now be a seven-time world champ—a claim that is always mentioned in his advertisements? If we let him get away with that, soon everyone else will jump on the bandwagon and start inflating their credentials, as well.

THE IDEAL FIGHTER'S PHYSIQUE

September 1999

The competitive martial arts are one of the most physically demanding endeavors on the planet. Consequently, becoming a champion fighter requires having or developing a certain physique that is a proven performer in the ring. Some of the essential ingredients are strong and fast legs, relaxed muscles, a strong neck, a favorable facial structure and a good overall build.

It is no coincidence that most great kickers have slender, light legs. Why? Because people with heavy legs become fatigued more quickly while trying to throw kicks. Also, it takes longer for a heavy leg to complete any kind of kick. A small, quick-legged fighter doesn't have this problem, because it's not the strength of the leg that counts; it's the movement. In other words, how quickly you contract your muscles to extend and retract your leg is what matters.

Big, bulky muscles can contract and become tight, and the buildup of lactic acid will make them feel tired and weak.

Why aren't more muscular, bodybuilder-type athletes involved in kickboxing? Because fast, small guys know how to relax their muscles. A relaxed muscle is a quick muscle. If you watch the fastest boxers of all time—Muhammad Ali, Sugar Ray Leonard and Sugar Ray Robinson—you will see that all three men danced all the time and kept their hands low. From that relaxed posture, they were better able to snap their punches. They knew that quickness was more important than raw power.

The best kickboxers recognize the same truth. Using speed, they can develop a certain amount of power regardless of how big or small their muscles are. Being strong is important, but so is being wiry. Big, bulky muscles can contract and become tight, and the buildup of lactic acid will make them feel tired and weak. That's why even heavyweight kickboxers aren't particularly muscle-bound. In a bout, a muscle-bound fighter may not last as long as a smaller fighter because his muscles just can't take the constant strain.

Having a strong neck is vital for a fighter because the neck absorbs the impact when a punch or kick lands anywhere on a fighter's head, whether in point fighting or full contact. It's like a shock absorber. Facial structure is also an important part of the ideal fighter's physique. Because of the way it reacts to a blow, a rounded or square jaw is better than a pointed jaw. Also, a large or hook nose can be a detriment because it will get hit more often and have a tendency to break or bleed. The eyes should be protected by a bone structure that does not have any sharp protrusions, which can lead to cuts. Some professional fighters even have surgery in which the bones around the eyes are shaved flat.

The ideal fighter needs to have a height that can support his weight. For example, there was a famous boxer in New York some time ago who was doing well in the ring. He was 6 feet 3 inches tall and weighed only 145 pounds, and he was absolutely wonderful—until he got clocked on the chin. He went down and never made a comeback. On the flip side, someone who is 5 feet 10 inches tall and weighs 300 pounds will have trouble fighting someone who is 6 feet 5 inches tall and 280 pounds. The ideal physique is a happy median between those extremes of height and weight.

The final attribute is having a fit and tough abdomen, topped by a pair of broad shoulders as a support structure. With all these physical qualities, a martial artist with good technique and stamina will be hard to beat.

CROSS-TRAINING IN OTHER SPORTS

January 2000

Participating in different sports and athletic activities can enhance the ability of martial arts practitioners. Weight training, biking, running, swimming, dancing and gymnastics are among the most helpful and popular physical endeavors for martial artists looking to supplement their *dojo* workouts.

One of the best exercises for developing power is weight training. Most martial artists should use light weights and high repetitions. They don't necessarily want to build bulk, because big muscles are less flexible and make it more difficult to move quickly.

Other sports that can help martial artists build upper-body strength include canoeing and kayaking; their indoor counterpart, the rowing machine, is also very effective. Another excellent exercise (one that is often overlooked in this age of specialized, high-tech machines) is the old-fashioned pull-up. It works the back, biceps and forearms, can be

done with minimal equipment, and does not require participation in an organized sport.

Martial artists, especially those who spar competitively, need to build their endurance, and this can be accomplished through biking, swimming and running. Running should not be confused with jogging, which is absolutely terrible for the knees, hips, ankles and insteps. Running at a sustained speed of 10 to 12 miles an hour, however, can be very beneficial. "Racewalking" can also boost endurance and build the muscles in the lower body.

Strength and endurance training can bump up the performance level of all martial artists, but those who practice the soft arts need something more. Dancing can provide immense benefits because it focuses on grace and fluidity without requiring much strength. This can help a kung fu stylist's performance by enhancing his agility. Dancing is also good because it is a form of exercise done to music, and music has been shown to help people relax. All martial artists need to remember that a relaxed muscle is a quick muscle—and one that is less prone to injury.

Gymnastics is another good cross-training sport with multiple benefits. Instead of forcing people to muscle their way through a movement, it requires them to learn the technique while remaining soft and flexible. At the same time, it can improve balance and develop fast-twitch muscle fibers. Certain aspects of gymnastics also develop the practitioners' explosiveness and fluidity of movement. The sport offers a special benefit to *taekwondo* practitioners because some of the kicks they do are similar to the movements used in somersaults, jumps and acrobatics.

Which of these activities would I choose if I had time for only one? Weight training with low weight and high reps. But I would be extra careful to avoid adding unwanted muscle bulk because that would slow me down—and that's one thing I don't want.

CROSS-TRAINING BOOSTS YOUR PERFORMANCE

January 2000

One style can't teach you everything you need to become a well-rounded martial artist. It's not enough merely to be able to execute a perfect spinning kick or to practice *kata* and know specific punches. You must also possess enough stamina to outlast your opponent and be strong enough to overpower him with a variety of solid techniques.

Cross-training in several martial arts can help you achieve all these things. Most martial arts classes last only an hour, and half of that time is typically spent warming up and doing basic techniques. Very rarely do you get to work on individual muscle groups in the *dojo*, and it's rarer still that you increase your heart rate for any substantial length of time. Training in different martial arts not only helps build your endurance but also helps you develop strength and flexibility in muscle groups that are unlikely to be used if you practice only one system. For example, flexibility and strength in the legs are important in both *taekwondo* and *shotokan* karate, but for different reasons: In taekwondo, you need to work on developing flexibility, speed and strength in your legs so you can kick; but in shotokan, you need strong legs so you can maintain low, driving stances.

Training in different martial arts not only helps build your endurance but also helps you develop strength and flexibility in muscle groups that are unlikely to be used if you practice only one system.

When developing a cross-training plan, you should try to find arts that you enjoy, as well as arts that complement what you are already studying. One way to do this is to read about them or watch a class given by a teacher of a different system.

Your instructor is a valuable resource in pointing you toward other arts. He might advise you to learn taekwondo techniques that will improve your flexibility or grappling moves that will increase your endurance. It's his job to present techniques from other systems that will give you an idea of what the styles are like, but it's up to you to take and modify these techniques so they work for you.

Anyone who wants to become a top-notch competitor or teach the martial arts should cross-train in different styles. The same goes for people who already have a good feel for different systems and want to try something new.

Ideally, you should have at least a green or brown belt in your first art before embarking on a cross-training regimen, because learning other systems too soon can be confusing. Cross-training is not ideal for very young martial artists. It usually takes one or two months of training in the second art before you start to assimilate the new techniques. But once you learn a few techniques from one or two systems, the rest will be easier.

Instructors now realize that adopting techniques from different styles can improve their own martial art. Consequently, more and more schools in the United States are doing just that. Cross-training keeps all martial artists thinking and moving. It helps them maintain their overall fitness, endurance and flexibility, and it helps build great muscular and cardiovascular endurance. Last but not least, it provides martial artists with a repertoire of fighting skills that can enhance performance in the ring. If you're not already cross-training, now is a great time to start.

HOOKED ON HOOK KICKS

December 2000

I am famous for my roundhouse kick. But because I have a bad right knee and fight from a left-leg-forward stance, I can't throw a rear-leg roundhouse kick. Therefore, it is ironic that the kick that works best for me is actually the exact opposite of the roundhouse: the hook kick.

The great thing about the hook kick is that it's effective as both an offensive and defensive technique. It's also very versatile, in that you can use it in combination with a number of techniques. For example, you can follow it with a roundhouse kick, a reverse punch or a left hook. Following a backfist with a hook kick has always been the most successful combination for me.

Just as there are differences in the ways martial artists block or defend against a kick, there are also differences in the ways they throw their kicks. My personal way of throwing a hook kick is different from the way others do it: Whereas most people step into the kick and keep their leg straight as they swing it through, I throw mine basically like a sloppy side kick. I keep my knee bent and snap my kicking leg out, but rather than snap it right back, I follow through so that I almost kick myself in my butt with my heel.

Following a backfist with a hook kick has always been the most successful combination for me.

One problem with the hook kick is that your opponent can step forward the moment you throw the kick and get inside your leg. Also, a lot of times when you start to throw it, he can tell right away what you're going to do. If you don't fake or disguise the technique by working it into different combinations, it will be easy to block and counter. One of my favorite ways to prevent this has always been to slide up, as if I were about to throw a roundhouse kick, and cock my leg right into the hook kick from that position. This strategy utilizes the knee a lot, which in turn increases the speed of the kick when I snap my leg.

For the kick to work, you have to be able to modify and play with the technique so you can make it go around or over your opponent's block. If nothing else, you should at least fake with a punch or kick so he lowers his hands.

The different fighting styles of your opponents can present problems when trying to execute the hook kick. I've found that the most difficult fighters to use it against are those who fight with their right side forward; I fight with my left side forward, and his hands are between my hook kick and his face. On the other hand, if my opponent fights with his left side forward, his shoulder will be in the way and my foot might get stuck on it.

To improve your hook kick, practice throwing the technique in front of a mirror. Aim at the reflection of your head, keeping your knee at shoulder height. When you whip the kick through, make sure your knee stays straight and level with your shoulder. The most important thing is to keep your knee up; if your leg drops, your upper body will fall forward.

Do this drill four or five times to see what the kick looks like, then start working on the heavy bag to find out how it feels to throw the kick at a target. You'll notice that it's fairly easy to throw this kick high, which is useful when you fight a larger opponent. You'll definitely want to work on your ability to get your leg up there with ease.

THE TRUTH IS OUT THERE

February 2002

The martial arts world is full of myths. They usually start when someone tells a factual story and, as the years pass and it's retold, it becomes more and more distorted until it bares little resemblance to the original account. This is not necessarily a bad thing. Regardless of whether the myths were ever true, they do give us something to think about and add depth to the culture of the martial arts. As long as there is a possibility that a spectacular event happened (or could happen), people have a reason to persevere in their training.

Many people say Bruce Lee died from a "death touch," supposedly inflicted because he showed Westerners the secrets of kung fu. That's bull.

The following are five of the most common martial arts myths and my opinions of them:

• **The reverse punch, when executed correctly, endows people with an almost superhuman "one punch, one kill" capability.** The reverse punch is just like a boxing punch, except it's thrown from the hip. Instructors claim it's the deadliest technique in the world, but when you throw it in a sparring match and nail your opponent in the ribs, he usually just bounces back and says, "Hey, good shot!" You didn't kill him, and you have to come up with an excuse, so you blurt out, "I controlled that punch pretty well, didn't I?" The truth is, you threw it as hard as you could, and it didn't do what it was supposed to. I believe the reverse punch is less deadly than it used to be because peoples' bodies change. The Chinese, Japanese and Koreans who used it centuries ago were not very physically powerful; somebody with big knuckles could throw a reverse punch and break a rib or puncture a lung, and the person might bleed to death. Today, people are larger, and medical advances have almost eliminated the risk of fatality when such injuries occur.

• **The karate chop has magical power.** No way. This technique is definitely a powerful one, and when it's thrown to the side of the neck, it can be very effective. But it's not as deadly as many nonmartial artists think. I remember witnessing a fight when I was in high school. One of the guys just stood there with his *shuto* (knife hand) held high, and alarmed bystanders whispered, "He knows karate. He's gonna hit that guy and kill him." Needless to say, nobody was killed in the skirmish.

- **A martial arts expert can touch a certain part of a person's body and kill him.** Many people say Bruce Lee died from a "death touch," supposedly inflicted because he showed Westerners the secrets of kung fu. That's bull. The people who believe stories like this also believe masters who say they can kill you if they want to, but they don't want to, so they're not going to. There is no spot on the human body that you can tap and kill a person.

- **A woman who has trained in the martial arts can beat a man who has not trained.** A woman can be victorious against a man only if she's got the element of surprise on her side or she is significantly stronger than her opponent. There are plenty of techniques a woman can use against a mugger who thinks she won't fight back; the woman can hopefully buy a little extra time to escape. But generally women are not as strong as men, and no matter what their game is—kicking, punching, grappling or whatever—if they hit a guy and don't do any immediate damage, they'll be in trouble.

- **If a person is a champion in the ring, he can easily knock out any opponent.** Not necessarily true. If you want to be a good fighter, you have to train the way you will fight. If you are going to fight full-contact, you have to learn to take the contact. Before I was a kickboxer, I was a national champion in point fighting three years in a row. I thought I was a super fighter because I could kick or punch my opponent and he couldn't hit me back. I never took into consideration the other guy's ability to defend against or absorb my strikes. That's why when kickboxing was born, kickboxers kicked butt against point fighters. The kickboxers could take a shot, and we didn't know what to do when we got hit. It takes a long time to psychologically and physically learn to take a punch.

THE SHAPE OF A MARTIAL ART
April 2002

I don't know of anybody who just woke up one day and said, "I want to take *shorin-ryu* karate," or "I want to take *goju-ryu*." Most people don't have any idea what makes one art different from the next. They just think karate is karate; it doesn't matter whether it's *taekwondo, jujutsu* or judo. They learn about those different systems only when they join a school and start reading books and magazines.

This is unfortunate, because many people end up studying an art that is not particularly well-suited to their body types and personal goals. Although they often discover whether they are gifted in the art they've selected or they should have picked a different style during their first three months of training, you can save yourself some time by reviewing the following guidelines for selecting a martial art.

• Because judo concentrates on throwing techniques, it's a good choice if you have a short, squatty physique. You won't be punching or kicking, so you'll have to rely on maneuvering close to your opponent, getting under his center of gravity and tossing him into the air and onto the mat. Judo is also a good choice if you are tall and lanky and don't want to wrestle or get down on the ground because you've got too many limbs in the way. However, even if you are highly skilled, you'll have trouble keeping a shorter opponent away from you.

It's essential to possess skill in kicking, punching and grappling—and once you find an art that suits your needs, you should work on filling in the gaps that exist in your arsenal.

• If you are small, you may want to study jujutsu, but you must not have an aversion to going to the ground, rolling around on your back and getting covered with sweat—both yours and your opponent's. While you struggle to get your opponent into position for an armbar or choke, you'll probably have to crawl between his legs and under his arms and contort your body in all sorts of directions. Having sustained a back or neck injury could preclude you from doing that.

• Taekwondo is best-suited for you if you're tall, slender and flexible. Those qualities will enable you to execute fast high kicks all day long. However, if you're heavily muscled or significantly overweight, you may find that your legs get awfully heavy after a while and that your kicks become slower and slower. You may also have to contend with poor endurance and flexibility.

• If you have a strong, stocky build, consider practicing shotokan or shorin-ryu karate. These arts will allow you to showcase your strong hand techniques and stances, and you can become very successful in competition and self-defense once you master them.

• Wrestling is a good choice if you are compactly built, strong for your size and have a good sense of balance and movement.

If you don't have one of the physiques described above, you should try a variety of arts to find out which one you like best. Also, think about which aspect of the martial arts appeals to you the most. I enjoy kicking, but you might prefer punching because you have a different outlook on fighting. Of course, it's essential to possess skill in kicking, punching and grappling—and once you find an art that suits your needs, you should work on filling in the gaps that exist in your arsenal. You needn't be an expert in every style of fighting, but you should at least be proficient in them.

Howard Jackson
Photo by Rick Hustead

SIX STEPS TO SELF-DEFENSE PROFICIENCY
October 2002

I find it a bit strange that so many people talk about self-defense techniques when the easiest way to protect yourself is to not be in a risky situation in the first place. When that's not possible, self-defense is about getting away from an attacker, not beating him to a pulp. Nevertheless, people desire to learn self-defense moves, so outlined below is a simple course for those who have no martial arts experience but want to be able to fight off an attacker.

Self-defense is about getting away from an attacker, not beating him to a pulp.

---

1. Ask someone who knows you well to assess your mental and physical condition. Are you afraid of fighting? Are you frail or weak? What kind of clothing do you wear when you're out? How strong is your will? That knowledge will help you determine how much emphasis you should place on developing your environmental awareness. If you're Superman, you can go anywhere and do anything you want. But if you're a mortal, you should learn where it's safe and where it's not safe to go in your city. Then you should adopt a lifestyle of avoidance and prevention: At night, walk only in well-lit areas. Look around before unlocking your car, and check the interior before climbing in. Examine your front door for signs of a forced entry before entering your home after work.

2. If you don't know how to throw a basic punch or slap, learn. After that, concentrate on the backfist. It's a fantastic weapon that can be thrown from either side of your body. To do it right, you must stand sideways with respect to your opponent before raising your elbow and pointing it at his face. Then snap your fist out and back. A blow to his nose will make his eyes tear up, temporarily blinding him. And if he can't see you, he can't grab you. Standing sideways to the attacker will allow you to turn quickly and run as soon as you throw the technique.

3. Learn how to perform the eye gouge and mentally accept that you may have to do something repulsive to save your life. Sometimes just poking an attacker's eyes is not sufficient; you might need to actually claw at his eyes or jam your thumbs into his sockets. Note that women are more likely to scratch than men; therefore, they may find it less objectionable to use their nails to defend themselves. Nevertheless, women often find the prospect of gouging an eye distasteful. They say, "I can't stick my fingers in his eyes" (until some guy starts ripping their clothes off, that is).

4. Perfect your knifehand strike. If somebody is reaching out to grab or punch you, you can slam a knifehand or two into his windpipe. That will make it difficult for him to breathe, and if he can't breathe, he can't chase you. True, the technique could crush his windpipe, but if your life is at stake, you shouldn't worry about that.

5. Focus on hitting the attacker once or twice so you can escape. Don't stick around so you can finish him off because you never know how many friends he has nearby, what kind of weapon he's carrying or how many drugs he's taken. If you stay and fail to hurt him or knock him out, he will hurt you.

6. Feel pain. All the aforementioned advice is useless if you freeze as soon as an attacker slaps you across the face or pushes you down. To avoid that paralyzing reaction, spend time in the *dojo*. Condition yourself to react instantly when your instructor or partner hits you. Think over and over about what you would do if you were punched, tripped, choked and so on. Try to make each response a natural movement, and seek help from your instructor if necessary. As you train, tell yourself, "My life is in danger. This guy is trying to hurt me. I don't mind if I poke his eyeballs out. I don't mind if I break his face." The more you fight in the dojo, the more comfortable you'll be fighting on the street.

ULTIMATE CROSS-TRAINING
December 2002

If you practice only your martial art, you risk getting burned out physically and psychologically. Your body will get used to doing the same techniques over and over, and you'll get bored. However, practicing another sport can help build muscle memory and develop hand-eye coordination and endurance. That not only will improve your martial arts performance, but also will renew your passion for your style. The following are some sports that can make a wonderful complement to your martial arts training.

Gymnastics is the best sport in which to cross-train. It's fantastic for martial artists simply because it requires considerable strength, agility and flexibility. Although it's not taught as part of a regular martial arts curriculum, many students take gymnastics to excel in *kata* competition. In fact, they often execute their forms exactly like gymnasts do their floor routines. For fluidity of movement, ballet or any kind of dance will improve your rhythm and teach you how to place your feet in the right place at the right time, but nothing beats gymnastics.

Gymnastics is fantastic for martial artists simply because it requires considerable strength, agility and flexibility.

Wrestling was probably the first martial art, and it's another great complement to your regular regimen because it forces you to be in tune with your body. To excel in it, you must be strong, in good physical condition and flexible. You also need to have the right attitude. A lot of times in the martial arts, people don't have the kill-or-be-killed instinct they need to succeed in competition or to defend themselves in a confrontation. In most martial arts classes, students never get hit very hard, so they don't know whether they can take it or not. In wrestling, however, athletes get thrown down, stepped on and twisted in ways they didn't know were possible. In the end, they find out they're not the "baddest" dude in the world—but they're also not the weakest, either.

Several other sports will boost your endurance and coordination. They include boxing, cross-country running, track-and-field and basketball. However, to reap the most benefits from any of them, you must learn to evaluate and trust your own abilities and attributes. If you are the worst player on a team that wins the state championship, you are still a champion. If you are the best basketball player and everyone else on the team is terrible, you still might not win the game. In football, bulk is advantageous because it can enable a big lineman to take out a player who is only 5 feet 8 inches tall. However, the opposite is often true in a fight: A bulky guy might be strong during the first few minutes of an altercation, but he'll get tired quickly because he's carrying so much extra weight.

Certain sports can be detrimental to the martial artist's mind-set. For example, although you might incorporate martial principles into your golf game, you're still playing on a course. Every shot is just about the same, and you learn to be conservative. In the martial arts, you are facing another human being. Each move will be a little bit different because you have to change the way you kick or stand in relation to your opponent. You don't have time to be conservative in self-defense.

Obviously, some sports have more direct benefits on your martial arts ability than others do, but it doesn't really matter what you take up, as long as it relieves stress and distracts you from your regular training. I can play 18 holes of golf and not mention the martial arts once, but afterward I'm likely to want to stretch and work out. On the other hand, I look forward to getting back on the links to relax after spending a weekend teaching a martial arts seminar. Above all else, when choosing a sport in which to cross-train, find one you enjoy. There is no benefit in doing something just because someone says you should.

TOUGH GUYS

March 2003

On September 29, 2002, a group of 13 boys—one of whom was only 10—and two young men allegedly beat a 36-year-old man to death in Milwaukee. After one of the teenagers reportedly threw an egg at the victim, probably as a prank, the man retaliated by punching another boy in the mouth, knocking out a tooth. The minute he did that, he was fighting a losing battle. The youths lashed out and used improvised weapons such as broomsticks, crates and other objects to bludgeon him to death.

We all have egos. Usually the first instinct when someone calls you a name is to come back and do the same to the aggressor. The man probably thought he would just pick a fight with the guy that threw the egg, and the other boys would leave him alone. Right. They were all friends; of course they would intervene and defend each other.

Unfortunately, there was probably very little the victim could have done to defend himself once that many people attacked him. His fatal mistake during the altercation was that he tried to be macho and stand up to the kids in the first place.

The martial arts are fantastic for defending against one or two people, but when you're facing 15 attackers at once, forget it. In that situation, the best thing to do is swallow your pride and try to talk your way out of the confrontation. You won't prove anything by beating up young kids. Pretending to be Billy Badass when you're facing 15 assailants will not help stack the odds in your favor. Even if the victim had been able to prevail, he probably would have gone to jail for assaulting a minor. He would have lost either way. However, if he had martial arts experience, he might have been able to talk his way out of an assault by simply backing down and saying, "Hey, I'm really sorry. You guys are right, and I'm wrong. Don't waste an egg on me. I'll just leave."

I think the reason I've never been in a street fight is because I don't stand around and argue with people. A one-on-one fight is one thing, but if there's a gang of aggressors involved, they've got the advantage right off the bat. If I hit one guy, I can be pretty sure his buddies will help out. While I'm busy working on one or two of them, there are bound to be a couple more right behind me, and I'll have no idea what they're doing. If they tackle me, I'll have only two weapons to fight back with once I am on the pavement: my hands. It's pretty tough to kick when you're on the ground.

Self-defense is about more than knowing which technique to use to fell an opponent. It's also about knowing where to be and where not to be so you can avoid getting in trouble. If you're in an encounter that might turn ugly, you should leave that environment. There's no law that says you have to stay in a dangerous situation.

His fatal mistake during the altercation was that he tried to be macho and stand up to the kids in the first place.

If you're ever attacked by a gang and can't get away safely, position yourself so all the attackers are in front of you. Then you can use them against each other. For example, grab one person, beat on him until he's weakened, then hold him between you and the other assailants. Use his body like a shield so the others have to get around him to get to you. If a group surrounds your car, don't get out. Start creeping forward so they have to move out of the way. They might beat on the car, but at least you'll be safe inside.

One thing I do know is that the group of boys who attacked that man in Milwaukee were wimps. If they really were tough guys, they would have evened the odds. They would have decided which one in the group would take him on, or perhaps the boy who threw the egg would have challenged him. But when 15 people with weapons jump on a single defender, their purpose is to kill—and they should pay the penalty.

FIGHTING BLIND

October 2003

You and your spouse are waiting for the bartender to take your order at a busy nightclub when a guy approaches. He pushes you and starts making lewd comments to your wife. The momentum of his shove takes you by surprise, and your eyeglasses fly off your face as you prepare to defend yourself. You feel blind. What do you do?

First, you need to realize that your glasses might be gone for good. They could get trampled accidentally or on purpose, or you might simply be unable to find them before the fight breaks out. But losing your glasses should be the least of your worries at that point.

The good news is that just about everybody who wears glasses can still see a little bit without them. However, your field of vision will probably suffer. You might misjudge distances. You might be unable to see anything clearly. You might have difficulty tracking objects that move quickly. None of those limitations will be easy to overcome.

I always advise martial artists to take off their glasses or sunglasses as nonchalantly as possible before someone who's trying to pick a fight can get close enough to make his first move.

To make matters worse, you might be injured by the kick or punch that knocks your glasses off. If you have glass lenses and one of them shatters, your cheek could be lacerated. If the frame is smashed into or dragged across your face, it could cut the bridge of your nose. If your opponent strikes you and transitions into a grappling technique that involves your head, the glasses could slice open the side of your face or your eyebrow region. The worst-case scenario would be if a lens broke and a splinter of glass flew in your eye.

I always advise martial artists to take off their glasses or sunglasses as nonchalantly as possible before someone who's trying to pick a fight can get close enough to make his first move. Avoid doing it in an aggressive way because the simple act of removing them can be interpreted as a sign that you're escalating the tension.

If you opt to leave your glasses on, know that it's very difficult to throw some techniques while you're wearing them—especially moves that involve a rapid turn. For example, when you do a spinning backfist, the first thing that spins is your head. If your glasses fly off at that point, you won't be able to see where your opponent is or how he might counter if you miss. Leaving your glasses on while grappling is also risky: When you drop and shoot in for a takedown or throw, the side of your head can crash into your opponent's leg, shoulder, elbow or knee. The resulting impact can easily knock them off and break them.

You have a few options for fighting with your glasses on, however. The side kick is one, because it allows you to keep your face away from your opponent. Your body is sideways with respect to his, so even if he manages to strike you, he'll probably just knock your glasses off your face and not into it.

Now, let's assume the shoe is on the other foot: Your opponent is the one wearing the specs. You can reach out and slap them off. The move will decrease his visual acuity and most likely distract him long enough for you to nail him with a follow-up technique—all without damaging his eyes.

If you wear glasses and want to be prepared for anything, practice defending yourself with and without them on. Devise scenarios in which they have been lost or damaged during an altercation. Have your partner swat them off your face to see what it feels like, and learn how to throw techniques when your vision is impaired. Experience what it's like to function during the few seconds it takes your eyes to adjust. And don't forget to practice smacking the glasses off your opponent. Better yet, use a training dummy to avoid the risk of injury.

SO YOU WANT TO BE A KICKBOXER...

December 2003

Contrary to what many people believe, a kickboxing match isn't just a brawl that involves walking into a ring and beating the heck out of somebody. It's very artistic, and training for a bout is almost a science. If you're interested in joining the ranks of professional kickboxers, here are some things you need to know to get started.

As a kickboxer, you must be able to take a shot. Most people think they're pretty tough until they actually get punched or kicked, and the first time it happens can be a rude awakening. If you've got a pretty face and don't want to get beat up, or if you don't have talent in the ring, kickboxing isn't for you. It can take a lot of time and hard work to become a champion, and it's a real bummer when you've been training for several years and suddenly realize it isn't the sport for you.

Most martial artists can fight well—for 15 or 20 seconds. When you start getting tired and the other guy keeps coming, it's not fun anymore. Your opponent will be like a bull that's constantly in your face, not letting you set up your combinations and putting pressure on you to wear you down. You need the endurance to deal with this kind of assault and a strategy for overcoming it. Sparring isn't just about seeing who the toughest fighter is; it's about seeing techniques that are coming at you, getting out of the way of some of them and absorbing others, and then countering. Professional boxers pay their sparring partners a lot of money to throw punches and kicks that an actual opponent will use just so they can practice blocking and countering.

Most up-and-coming competitors fight three to five matches a year and spend the rest of their time training. Therefore, you need to have people around you who support your goal to be a fighter and who will push you when you need it. You must also have someone who'll tell you what to do, when to do it and what's wrong with the way you're doing it. A coach or trainer will work with you on your physical conditioning and help you prepare for a match. You can find a good one by word of mouth or by making phone calls, but depending on where you're based, you might have to live for six months in a different state to spend time under his tutelage.

When you're ready to compete, your trainer will advise you which fights you should take because he probably knows your ability better than you do. If he doesn't also set up the matches for you, you'll need a manager to deal with the business side of your career. Don't call a promoter yourself, or he'll have you fighting for $10 a match. A good fighter can make $100,000 a year, but to get to that level, you need to build up the "wins" column in your record. You also need to develop a following so people will want to watch you compete and be willing to pay to do so.

Unlike other professional athletes, such as football players or golfers, kickboxers do not lead a glamorous life. They spend a lot of time in old, stinky gyms where people spit on the floor. They may have a lot of glory when they win, but they do not get sponsors because the sport is perceived as brutal. Also, a career usually isn't very long—maybe five or 10 years—because of the inevitable injuries. Indeed, the older you are, the longer it takes for bruises and cuts to heal. For this reason, coaches are always looking for "new blood" to replace athletes who are getting long in the tooth.

I recommend that you be at least 18 before becoming a pro kickboxer, but there is no specific age at which you must retire. I stopped competing at 35 because it was no longer fun for me, but Don "The Dragon" Wilson continues to fight a little, and he's in his mid-40s. If you're still interested in giving it a shot, go for it. It's a wonderful sport—probably the best thing I've ever done.

DON'T WASTE YOUR TIME
February 2004

If you've been in the martial arts for any length of time, you've probably been flooded with information about which punches and kicks work best for sparring. And you've probably discovered that you just can't execute some of them, no matter how hard or how often you practice. The natural question is, Should you spend your time trying to improve the techniques that don't seem to work, or focus on what you do best?

I believe you should determine which techniques work for you and concentrate on perfecting them. The following is my advice for coping with the challenge:

• **Choose three to six techniques you think you'll be able to use offensively and defensively.** Focus your training on them to determine whether they meet your expectations. If they do, practice until you can execute them without thinking.

• **Remember that no matter what anyone says, the key to victory doesn't lie in knowing scores of techniques.** Former world-champion boxer Joe Frazier had only one punch: the left hook. He would take all the punishment his opponents could dish out, then throw it and knock them out. Muhammad Ali used only the jab and the cross.

It's not necessarily a bad thing to be known for a particular technique. For example, I've always been good with a side kick. Long ago I learned that it's sometimes more fun if my opponent knows what I'm about to do and tries to counter it. It becomes a challenge to sneak it in—or nail him with a backfist coming over the top while he tries to block my kick.

• **Practice combinations composed of the movements that work well for you.** Every martial artist learns several basic sparring techniques; concentrate on them. The backfist is taught the first day of class, but that doesn't mean it's too elementary to work. The reverse punch, which is probably the second-most important technique you'll learn, is also taught right away—as are the roundhouse and side kick. Use them.

As much as people like spinning back kicks and jumping kicks, they seldom score in competition. Because they're so difficult to throw, you have to wind up before executing them, and that frequently gives them away. A skilled opponent will see what you're planning and stop you from doing it.

• **Speak up when your instructor or coach tries to make you spend time on moves you're not good at.** While I was competing, people often tried to get me to throw a right-hand reverse punch. Because I'm left-handed, it didn't feel natural. I could hit a heavy bag well enough with my right, but when an opponent was in front of me, I knew I'd be hit back if I threw a right-hand strike.

You'll be able to tell within the first month of training whether a move works for you or not by the way it feels.

• **If you find a new technique you like and believe it will enhance your repertoire, practice it.** Even if you have some problems executing it at first, it might still be worth working on for a while. If you later find it doesn't fit, move on to one that does.

Remember that when you begin training in an art, you learn just about all its techniques. When you test for black belt, you must demonstrate that you can do those techniques with proficiency. However, it's OK to feel comfortable with just a few of them, and those are the ones you should rely on in combat.

I believe you should determine which techniques work for you and concentrate on perfecting them.

THREE SUREFIRE SCORING TECHNIQUES
July 2004

In my February 2004 column, I explained why it's important to find a few techniques that work really well for you, which you can then polish and use in the ring. In this month's installment, I will identify three moves that I personally consider surefire ways to score.

The backfist is my No. 1 technique in point sparring because it's very safe to execute. It's also very difficult for an opponent to block because it's so fast. The backfist can be thrown from the same stance as the front-leg roundhouse and can be used both offensively and defensively. In the ring, anyplace the strike lands will score you a point.

I don't recommend that you use a backfist—or a jab, for that matter—if you're close to your opponent. The technique will not be strong, and if the other guy moves in close while you're trying to strike, he can come from underneath and clock you with a real strong counter of his own.

> *If you can throw even one technique well, offensively and defensively, it's almost guaranteed that you'll score.*

Next up is the front-leg roundhouse kick, a fine offensive technique and probably the easiest kick to execute. It's also very deceptive. The best time to do it is when you're moving into your opponent. Since your leg doesn't have very far to travel to hit a target and it's thrown from the side, you can fake it low or high. As you bounce up and down, you're not covering any distance, and he'll be busy trying to figure out what you're doing. He won't see you coming at him or know what your plan is until you blast him with the kick. You can also throw the technique several times in a row without losing your balance because the only thing you move is the leg you're kicking with. And when the kick lands, there's a definite, audible thump. Even judges who may not have seen you throw it will hear the noise and think, "That sounds like a point to me."

You shouldn't use the front-leg roundhouse if your opponent is standing sideways. As you throw it to his body or his head, he can get you with a hook kick because your side is wide open as soon as you extend your leg.

My final scoring technique is the front ridgehand, a great countermove that's primarily thrown to the chest, ribs and head. It's executed with the inside edge of your hand where your thumb is, not the meaty part near the heel of the palm. Unlike the backfist, the front ridgehand can be used when you're standing close to your partner. You don't want to throw it from too far away because, if you have to reach out for the target, the other guy can counter your strike.

These three techniques can also be used effectively in combinations. A good sequence might include the backfist and front-leg roundhouse. For example, if your opponent assumes a fighting stance, holding his hands in front of his chest, you can throw several roundhouse kicks to his stomach. As he lowers his hands to protect his midsection, you can unleash a backfist to his unprotected head.

The effectiveness of any technique depends on your distance from the target. When you set up one of these moves perfectly, your opponent won't be able to block or defend against it. Sparring isn't just about throwing a technique; it's also about defending against your opponent's counter. If I know when I throw something what my opponent has to do to hit me back, and I know how to defend against it, I feel more confident. Remember, if you can throw even one technique well, offensively and defensively, it's almost guaranteed that you'll score.

JUST WALK AWAY—IF YOU CAN

September 2004

L et me tell it to you straight: You never want to get in a bar fight. Things can get ugly in a hurry, and the person who comes in second could end up maimed for life. Or worse.

The most important measure you can take to avoid being in a bar fight is knowing where you should and shouldn't go at certain times. For example, if you walk into T.G.I. Friday's or the Hard Rock Cafe during the day, you're almost guaranteed that no one will pick a fight with you. However, if you go into a biker bar on a Saturday night and look at someone the wrong way, or say "hi" to the wrong person, you can be pretty sure a fight will start then and there.

If you ever find yourself in a tense bar fight, swallow your pride and try to defuse the tension before fists start flying.

Bar fights usually occur in the evening in poorly lit establishments, and they're usually spur-of-the-moment things in which one guy just nails the other, often for no real reason. Perhaps he accidentally bumped into the other guy and spilled his drink, or he cut in front of him in line while he was waiting to place an order. Maybe he and the other patrons didn't like the way the victim looked or the clothes he was wearing. If you ever find yourself in that kind of situation, swallow your pride and try to defuse the tension before fists start flying.

If a fight seems inevitable, you should immediately spring into action. Plan on hitting him before he hits you. But first, take a step backward to create more distance between you and him. The extra room will enable you to see what he's planning to do.

If you can't move back, step forward. That will confuse him and throw off any strategy that might involve using distance against you.

You should also turn your body slightly with respect to his. Don't put your hands up because that can be interpreted as an aggressive act. With your hands down at your sides, you'll be perceived as passive. However, you can throw a backfist at the guy and end the fight right there. Operating in a low-light environment can make your first strike easier to deliver.

If the aggressor is armed with a blade or club, grab a pool cue or beer bottle and try to knock the weapon out of his hand. Again, stand sideways to minimize the target you're giving him. Then, if you get hit, your arm will likely suffer the injury rather than a vital organ.

If he comes at you with a gun, your strategy should change. Your best chance hinges on just biting the bullet, so to speak, and apologizing for whatever transgression he thinks you're responsible for. Remember that it's tough to block bullets.

Often, your foe won't throw the first punch. Instead, he might shove you, in an effort to get you to swing first. In the eyes of most witnesses, the fact that he put his hands on you first is the same as hitting first. That means it's the best time for you to strike because, while his hands are busy pushing you, yours are free to act. Go for his eyes so he can't see. Hit him in the ribs or throat so he can't breathe. Or slam a side kick into his knee so he can't chase you. Then leave the establishment.

A caveat: If you use any martial arts techniques to defend yourself, the other person will say you "cheated" even if he's the one who started the fight. Furthermore, even if you thump him real good in the bar, he and his pals could wait for you outside, then finish the job by jumping you or damaging your car.

When you let a bar fight erupt, no one wins. In the best-case scenario, you'll beat up an intoxicated person. In the worst-case scenario, you'll be dead. Most people take up the martial arts so they can protect themselves, gain self-confidence and learn how to respect others. If you find yourself bickering over a brew, stay true to your training and just walk away.

DON'T LOCK OUT YOUR KICKS

November 2004

You can be injured while throwing any type of kick. That's a fact of life in the martial arts. But if you hyperextend your leg by locking out your kick, you can actually throw your knee out of joint, and then you'll be in a world of hurt.

In the *dojo*, you're most at risk when you thrust your leg out and let it completely straighten, especially when you fail to make contact with a heavy target. The injury is similar to tennis elbow, and it can sideline you for a long time.

Repeatedly hyperextending your leg stretches the ligament in the knee ever so slightly. Snapping your leg back compresses the cartilage in the knee and weakens the joint, allowing it to move around more. Once the cartilage can no longer absorb shock, you can easily throw your knee out of joint. Typical injuries include cartilage pulls and tears, as well as damage to the ligament.

Treatments vary. At the lower end of the spectrum, you might be advised to stay off your leg and keep your knee slightly bent. Or you might be told to rest and apply a hot or cold pack. At the extreme end, you might be scheduled for arthroscopic surgery to repair a torn ligament. Surgery can cost $20,000 or more, depending on the severity of the damage, and it can take six to eight weeks to recover. Even after your knee has physically healed, it might feel as though your leg is still weak. Therefore, the best course of action is to prevent injuries from occurring in the first place and, if that's not possible, to treat them while they're still minor.

The knee is not the only body part that can suffer when you kick improperly. Bones in the feet, ankles and toes can also be injured. People who practice *muay Thai* risk breaking their fibulae and tibiae because they throw hard, strong kicks in an effort to strike "through" the target.

Now that you're scared, it's time for the good news. I've been kicking for 42 years, and I've never hyperextended my leg or broken any of the associated bones because I don't really kick that hard. I just throw my foot out and snap it back, similar to how you throw a backfist. That protects the knee because the ligament snaps right back and the cartilage isn't compressed.

Another good way to protect your joints when you kick is to make sure you're sufficiently warmed up and your muscles are pliable. Every time you're ready to kick, first devote five minutes to a light preparatory workout.

Gradually work your muscles by separating your legs toward a split. Get your heart pumping to supply fresh blood to the areas being exercised. Unlike stretching, during which you try to elongate your muscles, warming up is a matter of getting your muscles flexible and ready to execute the moves without damage. I don't believe in doing ballistic (bouncing) stretches because you risk tearing the muscle and the fascia (the sheathing around the muscle).

If you want to incorporate kicks into your warm-up routine, don't throw them any higher than your stomach or chest. I like to start with a roundhouse kick because it's easy. Next, I do the side kick because it's a relatively low technique. Last, I practice the hook kick, which is my high kick.

There is no one best way to improve every martial artist's kicks. You'll have to find a method that works for you. Attack the problem gradually. After warming up, practice throwing your techniques at half-speed 15 or 20 times just to get used to the movement. Then start throwing them a little faster, harder and higher. If you experience pain, stop, and return to the level of intensity you were at before. Remember that the form, strength and speed of your kicks are more important than how high you can get your foot.

PROTECT YOURSELF

January 2005

Martial arts injuries are fairly common, especially when you start training. That's because when you're a beginner, you think you know how to execute your techniques, but chances are you aren't doing them correctly. In my November 2004 column, I discussed the injuries associated with a common mistake made by beginners: hyperextending the leg while kicking. The following are others that can crop up when you repeatedly move the wrong way:

• **Arms and elbows:** Hyperextending your arm is painful and inconvenient. Because you use your arms for so many things every day, you're unlikely to give an injured arm sufficient time to rest. Consequently, it can take a long time to heal. To prevent it from happening, make sure you snap back all your strikes. Never fully straighten and lock your arms when you throw a technique.

• **Back:** You can injure your lower back by twisting or turning the wrong way. The spinal cord has thousands of nerves running through it, and if you irritate one of them, it can cause a spasm. As your training progresses, however, you'll strengthen the muscles in the lumbar area and thus prevent most injuries. If you still find a way to strain your back, take a hot bath to relax your muscles.

Be mindful of what's going on around you; most of the time, martial artists get injured simply because they're careless.

• **Bruises:** They're usually caused when you block a technique or hit a target the wrong way. As painful as they may be, they usually go away by themselves.

• **Fingers:** A jam occurs when you twist your fingers and dislocate your knuckles while executing a technique. The injury is often seen in judo and *jujutsu* matches when an opponent jerks his sleeve out of your grasp. Since the left hand is typically used to grab and sweep an opponent, its phalanges tend to be the most vulnerable. You can also jam your fingers when you attempt to block in karate or kickboxing. The problem is often treated by pulling—or having a classmate pull—the afflicted digit to realign it. If a bone is sticking out where it's not supposed to be, however, you should see a doctor.

- **Hips:** A lot of people believe hip injuries occur because of kicking, but the real culprit is flexibility—or the lack thereof. When you warm up, make sure you stretch your inner leg muscles, called adductors. This will get the sinovial fluid to lubricate the joint and warm up the muscles so they're more pliable.

- **Neck:** Injuries to the neck often occur in judo and jujutsu because the practitioners are always trying to choke and neck-crank each other. Another cause is falling: If you hit the ground the wrong way, you can injure your spinal column. And a powerful blow to the head can fracture a vertebrae, slip a disc or pinch a nerve. To avoid these problems, build up your trapezius and neck muscles to support your head. Be sure to warm up to get your blood flowing.

- **Wrists:** There are eight bones in the wrist, and they can get cockeyed very easily. Whether you're sparring or training on a heavy bag, if you don't hit the target perfectly, your arm and wrist can bend the wrong way and leave you with a fracture, in which case you'll need medical attention.

While the aforementioned injuries are common, they are preventable. Always stretch and make sure your muscles are pliable before you start training. Remember that a relaxed muscle is not only a quicker muscle; it's also less prone to injury. Also, wear appropriate equipment—arm and shin pads, headgear and a chest guard—when you spar to protect your vulnerable areas. And strive to execute your techniques correctly. If you're a beginner, have another martial artist watch you so he can monitor whether you're hyperextending a limb as you throw a technique. Finally, be mindful of what's going on around you; most of the time, martial artists get injured simply because they're careless.

SUBSTITUTE TEACHER

March 2005

It's a great compliment when your *sensei* asks you, as one of his senior students, to teach a class for him. If it's your first time, it might make you nervous. Just remember that your instructor wouldn't have chosen you to fill in for him if he didn't believe you could do the job. The following guidelines will make the experience rewarding for you and your students.

Admittedly, the transition from being a student to instructing your peers can be nerve-racking and awkward the first time you do it. Nonetheless, you must act with confidence and demand the respect of your pupils. While you're the teacher, they must address you as "sensei," "sir," "mister" or "miss"—not by your first name.

You've got to impress the students, so unless your instructor has told you specifically what to cover, go over the moves you're good at. You don't necessarily want to teach what your sensei does, because you and he probably have different teaching styles. Unlike the student-teachers you no doubt had in high school, whose main job was to baby-sit the class, you know the material and you have something to offer the students.

A valuable strategy I learned in college is to first teach the students something they already know, then teach them something new. This keeps them happy because they feel confident with the familiar techniques, and it inspires them to come back to learn more new material at the next class.

> *You've got to impress the students, so unless your instructor has told you specifically what to cover, go over the moves you're good at.*

The most important thing to remember is that you must clearly convey the information. Rather than introduce a complicated move and risk giving them the wrong information, work on a simple self-defense technique, such as the backfist or front-leg roundhouse kick. Demonstrate it three, four or five times, then go through it at half- and three-quarters speed so they can easily see what's going on. Once they get the hang of each move, you can work them into a combination.

You should also explain why you're doing the techniques a particular way: Where and when do you throw a backfist or a roundhouse kick? Once the class understands these slightly more advanced concepts, make them practice the moves and combinations on each other.

If your sensei does order you to cover certain techniques during the class, you must follow his instructions. Start by doing warm-up exercises for 10 minutes, then go over the moves he asked you to teach for half an hour. You still might have an opportunity to add some spice into the lesson by having the class spend the final 10 minutes practicing variations of the moves.

When your sensei asks you to fill in for him, other students will generally accept it and elect not to give you a hard time during the class. Someone might resent it because he paid money to learn from the head instructor, not you. Maybe he's upset because he wanted to be selected to instruct, or maybe he thinks you're wasting his time. But if you calmly explain that your master asked you to run the class for him and that your job is to help everyone work on the material, that's usually enough to ease tensions and alleviate misgivings.

If one student insists on making trouble, try to correct him with individual attention. If that doesn't work, ask him to help you teach. That will usually straighten him out in a heartbeat.

PART 2

PERSONAL
HISTORY

WALLACE VS. HEARNS

February 1990

Thomas Hearns and I fought a three-round exhibition match on August 15, 1987 in Miami. The exhibition was on a Sunday, and Tommy and I worked out together the Friday and Saturday beforehand. He had a title fight coming up that October with Juan Roldan for the world middleweight boxing championship. Now, Tommy had never seen me, so it made me feel good that he picked me for the exhibition. When his people asked me what I was going to do, I told them I'd just go out there and kick him.

So Friday night we met, and we went over to the gym. I suggested that we suit up and spar for three or four rounds. Tommy's a tall man, taller than I am, and a very nice guy. He's got very long arms. So we're moving around the ring, nice and easy, with headgear and gloves on, and he throws a jab. Now, I've worked with some good boxers before, but I'd never been hit with a jab that stung like that one did. Well, I backed up and I went, "Damn!" Then I thought, "Now it's my turn," so I hit him with three or four hook kicks.

He had trained in Detroit with kickboxer Kerry Roop to get ready for our match, and he said, "Bill, you don't kick like Kerry kicks!" We kept working out and finding out more about each other.

Saturday, we went to the gym to spar again. We were getting ready, and just to screw Tommy up a little, I said, "You want to go a little quicker today?"

He said, "Fine."

So we're moving around, and I was watching him, and every time he threw his jab he was dropping his arm, so I was able to come in with a really good counter hook kick. Well, after I hit him with five or six counter hook kicks in a row, his trainer Emmanuel Stewart said, "That's it!" See, we weren't going to wear headgear for the exhibition, just gloves and pads, and Stewart felt there was no sense in Tommy taking a chance on getting cut when he had a title fight in October. That was fine with me, because I didn't want to get hurt either.

Tommy's got that mean right hand of his. He taught me how to throw a good right of my own. I found out that he throws the jab first and then comes in with the right hand, so I didn't try to come in on him or throw my jab. What I did was keep away from him and keep my left shoulder up. All I wanted to do was stay away from him and kick. I basically just wanted to survive because I was 42, fighting a guy who was 30.

In the first round of the exhibition, we wore headgear and 16-ounce gloves. We got in the ring, and he did his showboat thing and I did mine, doing the splits and such, and then we started. I threw a ton of kicks at him in the first round. Don Wilson was working my corner, and he said, "You know, you damn near threw 45 kicks!" Hell, I wasn't going to get hit with that right hand! So I kicked. Funny thing was, I caught him with a good counter left hook and buckled his knees. We played around the rest of the round and had a good time, and he punched me a couple of times with some good jabs. Everybody's worried about his right hand, but Tommy's got these long arms and this good, stinging jab.

In the second round, he caught me with a good right hand off a jab, and it put me against the ropes. It didn't hurt, but it was a good shot. But we were laughing and having fun, so he wasn't really trying to nail me, and I wasn't trying to nail him. Then he pushed me against the ropes and started doing this rope-a-dope stuff, and I turned him completely around with a hook kick to the side of the head. He looked at me, and I just smiled, and everybody in the audience started laughing.

In the third round, we settled down a bit. He threw a bunch of stuff at me, and I threw a bunch of stuff at him, and we were both getting a little tired. So we finished the last round, and that was it.

The nicest part of the whole weekend was when Stewart came up to me after the fight was over and said, "Bill, if you ever want to box, you just let me know, and I'll get you any boxing match you want."

I said, "Thanks, but no thanks." I've done that already.

That was one of the high points of my career, because Tommy Hearns is an absolutely fantastic person. He invited me to come to the fight that October, and I went, but I thought, "Hell, he meets people all the time. He probably won't even remember me."

After Tommy won the fight, I went to his room. He was walking down the hall, and he saw me and yelled, "Bill!" He took me to his room and there were his parents and his little girl and all his friends.

He introduced me to everybody, and his father came up to me and said, "Are you the one who kicked my son in the face down in Miami?"

I said, "That's me." Now, here it is, 15 minutes after Tommy has won his fourth world title, which had never been done before, and everybody's having their picture taken with me. It really made me feel proud. It was a high point in my life.

A TRIBUTE TO ERIC

April 1990

On October 27, 1989, my 17-year-old son Eric was playing defensive back for Ohio's Wheelersburg High School football team against Washington Court House in the final game of the season. As my son went to tackle one of their receivers, the other boy put his head down and both players hit head to head. Both of them went down for a moment, and then both the other kid and my son got up. My son was dizzy and left the field. He walked over to the coach and said, "Boy, I got dinged on that play," and a second later he was on his back in convulsions and seizures on the sideline.

At that time, no ambulance was at the game because another kid had gotten hurt about 20 minutes earlier, and they had taken him to the hospital. A doctor there, however, and he came over and looked at Eric, who was on his back and convulsing, already in a coma. The doctor looked down at him and said, "Aw, he'll be OK," and he walked away. I'd like to meet that doctor.

Anyway, they moved one team down to one end of the field and the other team to the other end of the field, just so they wouldn't see my son die. That's what they actually thought was going to happen. Finally, the ambulance came back, and I credit them with doing a very good job because they stabilized my son and took him to the emergency room. Washington Court House is a small town; it has an emergency room, but it doesn't have a hospital. So they cleaned Eric up and brought my ex-wife and her brother in to see him, basically to watch him die. He was still in a coma, but he wasn't convulsing anymore. The doctors were just going to let him die there and then cart him back to Wheelersburg.

Finally, owing to the begging of my ex-wife and her brother, they called Life-Flight, a helicopter service for people who've been in bad accidents and need immediate transportation to major hospitals in order to survive. Two hours after the initial injury, Eric was flown from Washington Court House to Grant Medical Center in Columbus. He was suffering from a subdural hematoma, which means you have a bruising of the brain, then the bruise hemorrhages. The blood pushed his brain to the left side of his head, which explains why the left side of his body was partially paralyzed when he woke up.

He was in intensive care and in a coma for two weeks. When he came out of the coma, they moved him to a rehabilitation center. He's walking around now, and he's regaining use of the left side of his body fairly well. His right side has always been fine. He's still got his cognitive thoughts. He can speak. He knows who everyone is. He doesn't remember the game at all, but he's progressing very, very rapidly.

The doctors had to drain the blood from his cranium; they drilled a small hole in his skull, but the blood started spurting out. They had to close it off because, when blood starts spurting out like that, parts of the brain often start coming out, too. So they open up the side of Eric's head to get the blood out and perform brain surgery. They also found and removed some damaged membranes.

I was in Toronto doing a seminar at the time of the accident. I'd like to note that the people up there were absolutely fantastic in getting me to see my son in time.

My son lost 49 pounds. All the muscles in his entire body atrophied through disuse. He's got to go through strengthening exercises and bulk up again. He's slowly gaining the weight back.

Full-contact karate scares me to death now. I got hit in the head, too, but it was fun. Now I've seen what a good, hard hit can do. Now I understand why some medical officials are out to ban boxing. All my son had to do was get hit once in the head. Wherever there could have been a tube, a wire, or a sensing

device, he had one—all over his legs, his arms, his chest, his head. What scared me to death was that they had a defibrillator stuck to the end of his bed. Those are the two things they put on your heart to get it going again.

My son was supposed to die. The doctor said he had a very small chance of living. I walked up to him and said, "Anything I've got is yours. My cars are yours, my body is yours, my ability is yours—anything is yours—if my son can just get up right now and walk away. What can I do for my son?"

And he said, "Nothing."

It was very scary. In the intensive care unit, they have what is called a "code blue," which means somebody just died, and it's announced over the loudspeaker. Everybody who isn't working with someone right then goes to that unit to try to get the person going again. My first night at the hospital, I'm lying there sleeping when I heard, "*Ring! Ring! Ring! We have a code blue, ICU! Code blue!*" I jump up, my ex-wife jumps up, and we run to make sure nobody's around our kid. As long as there's nobody around your kid, it's OK.

The martial arts really helped me stay calm in this situation because of my training and what I got in the full-contact ring—the pressure of getting hit, the pressure of knowing anything can happen. When people tell you they're not scared when they fight, something's wrong with them. Everybody who's ever fought has to realize that when you spar, there's a possibility that you can get hit just right and die. I'm all for kickboxing and full-contact karate. What I'm against is hard contact to the unprotected head.

You might say, "Aw, it will never happen to me." I didn't think it would happen to myself or my family. But after looking at my son, I don't want to ever hit anybody hard in the head again. I don't want to be the cause of putting someone in the hospital. It's just really scary.

As martial artists, we think we're tough, we think we can withstand punishment, we think we're pretty bad dudes. Well, you aren't bad when you're laying in that hospital with both arms strapped down. I thought I was tough, but after watching what my son has gone through in the last few months, he's much, much, much tougher than I am or ever was. If I lost a fight, big deal. I'd come back and find some way to beat you. But it's kind of hard to beat death, especially when you're right on the very edge and you've got half your head cut open. I'll never forget that. It really puts your priorities in line.

BILL WALLACE: THE EARLY YEARS

July 1991

I was born in the small Midwestern town of Portland, Indiana, in 1945. We later moved to Lafayette, where my father coached football, baseball and basketball, and also played golf professionally in the summer. You could say I grew up around sports.

Unfortunately, I was small. When I was a freshman in high school, I stood barely 5 feet tall and only weighed 89 pounds—your basic shrimp. That meant I was too little to play basketball or any of the other major high-school sports.

So when I was a freshman, I got interested in wrestling, because it has different weight divisions in which even little-bitty guys can compete. The problem was, there weren't any guys little enough for me because the lowest weight division was 95 pounds, so I had to wrestle against bigger opponents.

But I started wrestling and did fairly well. I was a good leg wrestler; I liked using the scissors technique and different types of pinning combinations that used the legs. I was also good at takedowns because I was pretty quick. Then, in my sophomore, junior and senior years, I grew—not much, but by my senior year I was all the way up to 127 pounds.

When I graduated, a friend talked me into joining the Air Force with him. I went through basic training, but I only gained 3 pounds. I was still short and wimpy.

Keep in mind that I had never seen or even heard of karate, full-contact or anything like that. I'm from a small town in Indiana; there probably wasn't a single karate school in all of the Midwest at the time. When I got to my permanent duty station, I went to the gym and asked if they had a wrestling program. The guy there said, "No, we don't. The closest we have to wrestling is judo."

This guy I had been talking to happened to be the judo instructor. He asked if I wrestled, and I said, "Yes, sir."

So he said, "Let's wrestle." We went onto the mat, and I took him down, pinned him and beat him. Then he said, "That's pretty good. Now put on this little white jacket." So I put on the little white jacket and found myself being put into orbit several times. He was throwing me all over the room. Every time I tried a wrestling move, he'd just grab me and put me in a choke hold or an armbar, or he'd drop me on my butt. I asked what that stuff was, and he told me I had just been introduced to judo.

I really liked judo, so I started working out with their team. I did very well, at one point taking second place in my division at the Air Force team championships—as a white belt. Then, in 1966, while I was getting ready for the California State Judo Championships, a guy fell on my right knee and tore the medial collateral ligament. Just like that, my judo career was over. *Kaput*.

I liked karate because you could throw your opponent and didn't have to let him up.

They put me in a leg cast for several months. As I'm walking around in this cast, a friend tells me a karate school just opened down the street. We checked it out and talked to the instructors. Two guys named Mickey Geneck and George Torbett became my first karate instructors.

I liked karate because you could throw your opponent and didn't have to let him up. In judo, you throw the guy, let him up, throw the guy and let him up. Karate seemed more realistic.

Bear in mind that I had never been in a fight in my life. Even as kid, no one had ever whomped on me. I was afraid to get hit in the face. I thought that if you got hit in the face, your nose got splattered all over the place, your face caved in and it hurt like hell. I didn't want to put up with pain. So when we were learning karate, and I was trading punches with a partner, I didn't like it. Then we did front kicks, and I didn't like those either, because I couldn't use my injured right leg. But then we started doing side kicks, and I thought, "Hmm, I like this." And then we started doing front-leg roundhouse kicks to the body, and I said, "I *really* like this."

George and Mickey taught me *shorin-ryu* karate. I still had the torn ligaments, but I worked out anyway. I got out of the cast and that same month I went to a karate tournament, even though I was only a white belt. I wore my judo *gi* and my judo brown belt, and I competed in the brown belt division. This was my first karate tournament, and I took second place in my division.

My two main kicks were the side kick and the roundhouse to the body. While I was at the tournament, I watched other people throw their front kicks to the stomach, and I thought, "Look at this: That guy kicks him, and the other guy drops his hands to block. Why can't you start to throw that midlevel kick, and then just throw it higher?"

The first combination you learn in karate is the high backfist and the low reverse punch. It's the same theory: Make the opponent bring his guard up, then nail him low. I asked myself, "Why can't I throw the kick a couple of times to the body—*Bam! Bam!*—start to throw it again, and then go to the head?" So I started playing around with high kicks. In fact, the first time I tried it against my instructor, I hit him smack in the face.

To this day, anybody who attends one of my seminars learns the same principle. I throw the kick so you block it. When you block it, somewhere else you're open. It's up to me to find that opening. When I throw my combinations, they're designed to find openings. And the beauty is that you don't know if the kick is just a setup or if it will score.

I learned all the forms and did the competitions and everything in nine months, and I earned my shorin-ryu black belt. Soon afterward, I got out of the service and eventually attended Ball State University. It was at Ball State that I met Glenn Keeney. We became close friends, sparred together and attended many tournaments. Glenn had a substantial impact on my life. He's the one who eventually led me to become a professional full-contact fighter, and he's the best friend I've ever had in karate.

THE BEGINNING OF FULL-CONTACT KARATE

August 1991

I enjoyed fighting in point karate tournaments, but I was always afraid to get hit in the face. That's why I used a lot of combination kicking, because at a distance, I can still kick to the face without getting punched. But if I'm close enough to punch you, then you're close enough to punch me back. And that hurts.

Besides, if I wanted to box, I would have gotten into boxing. I've always said since day one that kicking somebody in the head made me feel good. Then came full-contact karate.

I was teaching karate in Indianapolis in 1974 when Joe Lewis called and told me about the first full-contact championship card. He had Mike Anderson, Howard Jackson and Jeff Smith on the phone with him. "Guess what, Bill?" he said. "We've picked you as the middleweight for our team."

"Wow!" I said. "What tournament are we going to?"

Anderson explained, "We're having a full-contact world championship tournament that will air on ABC."

"What did you say?" I asked, just to be sure.

Anderson said, "We're having a full-contact championship, and we've picked you as our middleweight."

I said, "Hey, thanks, but no thanks. I'm not going to fight anybody and have him punch my lights out." But they wouldn't listen to me.

Lewis said, "Wallace, you're it. Enough said. We've called you, and we've let you know that you're it."

This was in February, and shortly thereafter I moved to Memphis, Tennessee, to run a school for Elvis Presley. I tried to forget the phone call, but in May, these guys called me back and said, "We're going to Germany at the end of the month. There's a big tournament over there, and we want to go and fight as a team." So I agreed to go. Our team consisted of Lewis, Smith, Jackson, myself and Jim Beaver as our alternate. I started thinking I could do this.

When I went back to Memphis, I started working out. I had no idea what I was doing; I didn't know anything about boxing or full-contact. But I knew how to get in shape endurance-wise, so I started running, pumping weights and punching the bag. I had a friend who was a boxer, and he taught me how to throw the left hook, the right hand and the jab. I started sparring with him, and I learned right off the bat why I didn't want to get punched. It hurt.

But after you get hit three or four times, I discovered that the shock of being hit wears off. I didn't die. My eyes didn't pop out, and my nose didn't break in 18 places. Sure, it hurt, but it didn't *hurt*. Like stretching, it was a pain you could get used to.

Well, September came along, and I went to this big full-contact tournament Lewis had dragged me into. I think there were four teams: Japan, Canada, West Germany and the United States. Basically, I was still a point fighter. Actually, we all were, except Lewis. He was the only one who knew how to throw things hard.

My first match was with a West German named Bernd Grothe. I get out there and I bow in against this Grothe, and he just starts running from me. I caught him with a couple of kicks, but I kept a distance from him because I didn't want to get hit. Then he tried to sweep me. My counter for a sweep is just a defensive hook kick. I let him pick the leg up, and I reached around and stuck him with it. It caught him flush on the face and knocked him down. Grothe got up by the count of eight, but in those days a knockdown ended the round. In the third round, I dropped him again with a side kick to the body. That was the end of the fight and I won.

No matter what happens, I'm a karate person, and that's the secret of my success.

That put me against Canadian Daniel Richer for the world middleweight championship. He was a tall, thin, slender guy, but a very good kicker. He threw some good kicks at me, but I'm sneaky; I got away from them. Then he came in with a roundhouse kick. I grabbed the kick, took him down and punched him, winning the round. In the second round, I knocked him down with a roundhouse kick to the head, so I won that round and the match.

That made me the world middleweight champion, but I never felt like a world champion. I figured it was just another tournament. But I kept at it. I later fought Joe Corley and then Blinky Rodriguez. I started getting better and better.

I went on to become one of the most recognizable full-contact fighters of all time. That's because I still used karate. If you look at Rodriguez, Benny "The Jet" Urquidez, or Don "The Dragon" Wilson, they're always in boxing stances. But if you look at Bill Wallace, the leg is up and ready, and I'm in a sideways karate stance. No matter what happens, I'm a karate person, and that's the secret of my success.

MAKIN' IT IN THE MOVIES

November 1992

I've said several times in the past that I don't care much for the movie business. I have no problem *watching* movies, and I like working on a movie for about the first two weeks. You get to meet new people, read a new script, and come up with exciting fight scenes. But it gets old really fast.

The average movie takes three or four months to film. There's a lot of repetition and a lot of hard work. We might have to film a particular fight scene, or various segments of a fight scene, dozens of times to get all the right camera angles and get the continuity right. And that's very tiring, physically and mentally.

John Belushi, with whom I did some film work in *Continental Divide* and *Neighbors*, gave me the best piece of advice I've ever heard about making movies. He said, "Bill, when you sign up to work on a movie for three or four months, you might as well just erase those months from your life. Because for those months, you won't have time for anything but the movie."

He was right. That's why, once an actor gets established, he only makes one movie or so every year or two. It takes awhile to recuperate after each one.

Everything I know in the martial arts film business I learned from Chuck Norris. My first movie experience came in 1978 on *A Force of One*. Chuck called me and asked if I'd like to be the bad guy in the movie. I met the producer and the crew, and somebody told me, "Don't worry, you're not going to die in the film. The bad guy escapes at the end." So I decided I'd try it out. Well, by the middle of the film, I'd already killed several cops, I was running a drug trade, and I'd killed Chuck's son! There was no way I was going to escape alive. Sure enough, Chuck caught me and broke my back in the movie.

Working with Chuck and his brother Aaron, I learned about camera angles, continuity and good fight choreography. I was nervous at first, especially working with Chuck on the fight choreography, but he showed me what he did, and I started picking up on his techniques. We have different builds, of course, and my kicking style is different than his, so I gradually started shifting my parts of the fight to the way I move.

Playing the bad guy in *A Force of One* set a precedent for me—either that or my face is the type that makes people want to kill me. Whatever the reason, in all the movies I've appeared in, I've played the bad guy, and I've always died.

In 1984, I did a film with Jackie Chan. That was a lot of fun. I played the bad guy, of course. We had to film an American version and a Chinese version. The plot didn't really change, but all the fight scenes did. The reason for this is because Americans like to see big brawls with knock-'em-out slugfests, while the Chinese like acrobatic jumping and flashy fight scenes.

I've enjoyed almost everyone I've worked with in the 14 movies I've been involved with. That's pretty amazing, considering how many actors out there have really big egos and can be easily offended.

I recently did the fight choreography for the movie *The Power of One*. Working on that film reminded me of all the reasons why I hate making movies. I spent months in Zimbabwe teaching Morgan Freeman, Stephen Dorff, Daniel Krieg and Bobby Reed how to box, and the director, John Avildsen, edited all the fight scenes out of the final cut. It was a two-hour boxing movie with less than 30 seconds of fight scenes. I guess the director wanted to make an artsy drama out of it, but I think he made a mistake. It

was in theaters for about two weeks, and then the studio pulled it so they could make some changes to it.

I also had a big disagreement with Eddie Stacy, the stunt coordinator on *The Power of One*. He wanted to choreograph a brawl in which the lead character, played by Dorff, is beaten senseless for 20 or 30 seconds by an evil police officer. So Dorff gets hit 15 or 20 times in the face, gets up, shakes his head, hits the police officer twice and knocks him out. Come on! That's one thing I hate about martial arts movies. The star can be beaten senseless, then throw one or two punches and win the fight. Or a lot of times, he beats up 15 guys in 15 seconds. It just doesn't work that way in real life.

And just because you're a good martial arts actor doesn't mean you'll be a good fighter in real life. And just because you're a good fighter, don't think that will translate straight into movie fame.

I don't want to disillusion anyone out there who wants to try to make it in the movie business. The money is very good and, basically, they're paying you a lot of money to do very little. It just takes a lot of time out of your life, and you have to live with another person telling you what looks good and what doesn't. It's just not for me.

THE OLD, GRAY BILL AIN'T WHAT HE USED TO BE— BUT HE'S STILL BETTER THAN MOST

March 1996

When I was 25, I had visions that I was going to be champion of the world. I'm sure many other martial artists had that same vision. We would train three or four hours a day and really push ourselves. We knew that if we pushed ourselves, we were going to get better, stronger, faster and develop better technique. There was only one way to go, and that was up.

Then we suddenly get older and have added responsibilities—career, marriage and family, or maybe our focus just changes. Your priorities and commitments change. Pretty soon, the three hours you used to set aside for training gets trimmed to one hour.

I think that, as we get older, our competitive spirit often diminishes a little bit. And in some cases, a lot. I'm 50, and I've been in some sort of competition since Little League baseball, Pop Warner football, you name it. If you've been in some sort of competition since you were 5, that gets very old. I still love to play golf. But I don't like to play with guys who want to play for money. Once I'm playing for money, it's competition again.

I'm 50, and there isn't a day that's gone by that I haven't thrown a kick or a punch or done some type of martial arts training.

When we get older, we realize that we still have to work out. But now all we try to do is maintain a certain level rather than get better, because we know we're not going to get any better. I don't have the same elasticity, movement, strength, speed or power that I had at 25 or 30. The body gets old and starts to wear out. Maybe I'm smarter and have more experience, which allows me to compensate for some of the things I've lost through aging. But I don't have the same tools that I had back then.

What I do have is the ability and desire to work out. So now, instead of trying to get better or perfect my technique, I simply try to maintain what I have. I feel very good to still be able to do splits at my age. And I still do the same kicking techniques and combinations.

A word of caution: When you're coming back after a long absence

Photo by Rick Hustead

from training, take your time. I've talked to people who've been out of the martial arts for three or four years because of injuries or other commitments, and they want to go back and train. My advice is to start easy and take your time, like a new student. A lot of guys come back and expect to do perfect side kicks, roundhouse kicks and punches. You are not going to be able to do it. Your muscles won't remember how. Start as if you were a beginner again.

You have to worry about how much punishment your body can take as you get older. And you have to worry about the nagging injuries. Some injuries won't go away because you don't give them the chance to go away. And the older we get, the longer it takes injuries to heal. Older people should avoid any kind of straining of the back, as well as taking shots to the head or to the shoulders.

My physiology teacher told the students the first day we came to class, "The very second you come out of the womb, your body starts to deteriorate. You don't grow, you just start getting older."

I'm 50, and there isn't a day that's gone by that I haven't thrown a kick or a punch or done some type of martial arts training.

When older folks compete and win trophies, I think that's great. It's great to see their excitement and enthusiasm—not necessarily because they win trophies but because they go out and show everybody, including themselves, that they can still do it. You'd be surprised at what pride can do for you.

My advice to older martial artists is to have fun; have an absolute ball when you work out. By training, you're keeping your body in good physical shape and building muscle memory. When young guys look at you and say, "Wow, I want to be able to do that when I get to be your age," it'll make you feel good.

BEFORE THERE WAS "SUPERFOOT" THERE WAS... "SUPERWIMP"?

May 1996

When I was a little kid, I didn't know what karate, judo or any of the martial arts were. I grew up in a small town in Indiana called Lafayette, where my father was a junior high and high-school football, basketball and baseball coach, as well as a golf instructor.

My father gave me just about anything I wanted. I wasn't spoiled, but I guess I'm one of those few people in the world today who had a really happy childhood. My father and mother never beat me. I wasn't sexually abused. I got to go to the movies on Saturday and Sunday. I had friends over, and I wasn't locked in my room every night and forced to do homework. I was given an allowance, but I had to help out around the house. My parents, who are still alive, are two of the most wonderful people you could ever meet in your life.

It was a situation where, if I won, I got all the glory, and if I lost, I had nobody to blame but myself.

I was sort of a little wimp in high school. I wasn't a nerd, but if there were 50 people in the class who were tough, I wasn't one of them. I was picked on a lot growing up. When you're in your senior year of high school, it always seems like there's some junior, usually quite big, who wants to pick on a senior. During my senior year, I was the one the big junior wanted to pick on. It's still the only street fight I've ever been in. But it wasn't really a fight because I only hit him twice. I hit him with two left hooks and knocked him out.

As a youth, I was very shy. When I was in high school, if I had a speech to give that day, I would stay home and pretend to be sick. I couldn't get up in front of people. I was afraid, scared and shy. I dated one girl my senior year; I had about five dates with her and that was it.

I guess I started in the martial arts in junior high school, when I weighed 89 pounds. When you're under 5 feet tall and weigh 89 pounds, you're not going to be on the basketball team, and you aren't going to make the football team. Your chances athletically are very limited. I didn't like to run, so track was also out.

However, they had a wrestling team, and when I reached the ninth grade, the wrestling coach invited me to join the team. I wrestled in the 95-pound division because that was the lowest weight class. I had a total of one wrestling match my freshman year, and I won by pinning the guy.

I really liked wrestling because it was a one-on-one confrontation. It was a situation where, if I won, I got all the glory, and if I lost, I had nobody to blame but myself. When I was a sophomore, I had ballooned all the way up to 103 pounds. I started playing around with leg wrestling, like the scissors hold they do in professional wrestling, except we tried to pin guys rather than hurt them. I got fairly proficient at that, and in my senior year, I was the only one to beat a defending state champion.

When I got out of high school, a friend talked me into joining the United States Air Force. I wanted to continue wrestling while I was stationed at Fort Smith Air Force Base in Michigan, but they didn't have a wrestling team. They did, however, have a judo team. The odd thing was, I could beat the judo instructor because, when he came in for a throw, I would just take him down with a wrestling takedown—a double-leg, single-leg, fireman's carry, something like that. I would be able to pin him, and I was still a white belt at the time. As a team, we won the Air Force judo championships.

In November of 1966, after receiving my brown belt in judo, I tore the medial collateral ligament in my right knee and had a cast from my crotch to my ankle. Obviously, I had to put judo on hold for a while, but a friend told me about a karate school downtown and asked if I wanted to go take a look. I said, "Sure." I thought the karate school was really neat, so I began working out there even though my leg was still in a cast. Since my right leg was in the cast, I did all the kicking drills with my left leg. It was fun.

Probably the best thing that ever happened to me was when I enrolled at Ball State University in 1967, after I got out of the service. My first year there, I met a karate instructor in town named Glenn Keeney. Glenn taught me how to set up my opponent, how to create and how to best use my skills.

MAKE A KICKBOXING COMEBACK? THANKS, BUT NO THANKS

August 1997

Very few fighters who attempt comebacks are successful. Joe Lewis made a mildly successful comeback in professional kickboxing while in his 40s, but not against top-notch competitors. Most comebacks end badly.

You have to realize that there is a reason the fighter quit in the first place. Take Sugar Ray Leonard. He had won everything there was to win, and then he lost a fight so he decided to retire. He had started a family and had other things going on. His priorities changed. But he missed the money and the attention, and he came out of retirement several times, which was a big mistake. Muhammad Ali kept coming out of retirement, and even though he was tough, he took a lot of punches he really didn't need to take at the end of his career.

Lewis was a fantastic kickboxer in his prime. He's one of those guys that I would want on my side in a fight. But you have to realize that, when you reach a certain age, your skin stops becoming elastic. And Lewis, because he's blond, blue-eyed and fair-skinned, has somewhat thin skin. If he gets hit around the eyes, he's going to split open and cut. And that's what happened to him in some of his comeback fights. He didn't lose any fights by getting knocked out, but he got cut and the officials stopped the fight.

If a fighter is going to make a comeback, he must do so within a certain range of time after his retirement. Leonard recently came back after too many years in retirement and suffered an embarrassing loss to Hector "Macho" Camacho. A fighter's priorities in life change, but then someone encourages him to come back and assures him he can do so successfully. So the fighter starts training, and although he may appear to be the same as he was before he retired, he's not.

I'm 51. I still feel good, and I'm still as flexible as I ever was. I can still kick, but maybe not as strong or as fast as before. I still love to work out. But now I also like to play golf. Rather than go to the gym and beat on a heavy bag for 15 rounds or spar, I like to play 18 holes of golf. Most former pro fighters still train to some degree, but in the back of their minds, they're probably thinking, "I'd rather be doing something else." They're tired of dieting and just want to go out and eat whatever they want.

During my college years, as soon as my studies were done, I immediately headed to the karate school to spar. All I wanted to do was spar. Now I don't want to spar anymore. The bruises last longer, and it's just not as fun as it used to be. But I still like to stay in shape. As you get older, your priorities change and your life becomes less one-dimensional.

My father was a coach, and I was consequently always around sports. Since I was about 5, I've competed in some type of sport, whether it was baseball, basketball, football or wrestling. Even while I was in the military, I wrestled and competed in judo, and I later started competing in karate. I retired from professional kickboxing when I was 35, so for 30 years I'd been competing against somebody for something. It just got old. It stopped being fun.

Making a comeback at 40 never even entered my mind. For one thing, I never wanted to get hit. Another motivating factor came when I fought Emilio Narvaez in 1978. I caught him with a left hook in the first round and could see he was in trouble, so I tried to finish him. He struggled back to his corner at the end of the round, and I was sure I was going to get him in round two. But this 19-year-old fighter seemed to magically heal between rounds, and he came out fighting harder than before. That was enough for me. I retired the next year. I'll only come back now if I can use a putter in the ring.

A DIFFERENT SIDE OF "SUPERFOOT"

October 2001

Black Belt: When and where were you born?

Bill Wallace: I was born on December 1, 1945 in Portland, Indiana.

BB: What was it like growing up there?

Wallace: It was a small town. There were probably about 5,000 people. It was nice. My father was the head coach of the high-school basketball, football and baseball teams. Basically, I had it made. I got to go everywhere with him.

BB: At what age did you start your martial arts training?

Wallace: I started when I was 18. However, when I was 14, I started wrestling in high school because I was too little to play basketball or football. When I was a freshman, I weighed 89 pounds.

BB: Why did you decide to go into the martial arts?

Wallace: A friend talked me into joining the Air Force right out of high school because we didn't know what we wanted to do. When I enlisted, I wanted to wrestle, but they didn't have a team. There were, however, some funny-looking guys with white pajamas running around and throwing each other all over the place. So I said, "Hey, what is this stuff?"

The guy said, "It's judo."

I said, "Well, I don't know anything about judo, but does anybody here wrestle?" The judo instructor was a wrestler, so I wrestled him and beat him.

BB: What do you remember most from those early days?

Wallace: I used to get the tar beat out of me. The good thing about being young is that you heal quickly. During my judo training, I dislocated both shoulders, banged my knees and fingers, and suffered black eyes.

BB: What was your proudest martial arts moment?

Wallace: I guess it was during my first year on the Air Force judo team, when we won the team championship. The following year, I finished third in a pool of about 20. After that, I tore my knee. That's why they now call me "Superfoot" and not "Superfeet."

BB: As a youngster, was there anything you didn't like about the martial arts?

Wallace: Forms. When we were doing our little song-and-dance routines, I used to think, "There's nobody here. Why do I have to punch hard?" Then I'd turn my head and throw a kick real hard and wonder why again.

BB: Did you participate in other sports?

Wallace: I wrestled in high school and college, I played baseball in high school, and I was the center on the junior high football team.

BB: Were there any sports you weren't good at?

Wallace: Track and tennis. In tennis, I either hit the ball too hard, too soft or in the wrong direction.

BB: Who is the most influential person in your life?

Wallace: My father. Thanks to him, I was always around sports. He was always coaching football, basketball, baseball or golf.

BB: When martial artists begin training, they almost always learn about tradition. Now that you've been in the arts for a while, what are your thoughts about traditionalism in the arts today?

Wallace: Tradition is important. Everyone should have an understanding of his art's history. Sure, hundreds of years ago reverse punches used to do some damage. However, things change. Everything is different now. Back then, people weren't as strong as they are today. They didn't train as much as we do. We're much stronger than we were 100, 200 or 300 years ago. We're bigger, stronger and faster, and we heal more quickly. What worked before won't necessarily work now. Therefore, the kicking and punching techniques have to be changed. They must be updated.

BB: Did you always want to be a martial artist?

Wallace: I didn't even think about it until I went in the Air Force. I just played judo because it was fun. When I got out of the service, I went to college and wrestled and played judo. By then, I had started karate, too. After I graduated from college, I taught karate, judo and wrestling at Memphis State University. When I graduated from Memphis State, Elvis Presley hired me to work with him. Then Kenny Newton hired me to teach at a karate school in Indianapolis. Now I just travel around doing seminars, exhibitions and films.

BB: How long did you train with Elvis?

Wallace: From 1974 to 1977. I ran a school for him, and my job was to work out with him. Other times we'd just hang around.

BB: What was he like?

Wallace: He was a real nice person. A good old country boy.

BB: Do you have any heroes in the martial arts?

Wallace: Gene LeBell. He's the most wonderful person you could ever meet in your life. Sure, he's the ugliest guy in the world (*laughing*), but he's just a doll. And he looks good in his pink uniform!

PART 3

COMMENTARY

MUAY THAI: MARTIAL ART OF THE '90s?

January 1990

Martial arts in the United States have gone through several phases. First there was judo in the '50s and early '60s. Then karate came along, and after karate came *taekwondo* in the late '60s and early '70s. In 1973, kung fu came along, with the rising popularity of Bruce Lee's movies and the *Kung Fu* television series. Then, all of a sudden, full-contact karate arrived in 1974, which flourished until about 1978 or 1979. In the '80s, we had ninjamania, which lasted until about 1985.

Now the big thing is *muay Thai*. I was recently in Europe, Australia and New Zealand, and everything there is muay Thai now. They don't want to actually fight using the Thai leg kicks, but they want to train with them. A lot of people now are interested in leg kicks, their effect, how to set them up, that sort of thing. They don't want to use muay Thai in sparring because nobody wants to get injured, but they want to know how to do it because leg kicks work well in self-defense situations.

Personally, I don't like leg kicks, and I think the inclusion of leg kicks is the reason muay Thai won't ever become big in the States. Why? Leg kicks are designed for one purpose only: to injure the leg so you can't continue fighting. That's it, cut and dried. And in America, that's usually considered dirty fighting.

Plus, muay Thai training is very, very hard on your body. Talk to any muay Thai fighters who have been over to Thailand, and they'll tell you. Professional Thai boxers' careers last about four years. Your legs have all kinds of blood vessels and capillaries in them. If they keep getting beat on, like they do in muay Thai training, you get blood clots in your legs. And if a blood clot starts moving, it can kill you.

I work out at Benny Urquidez's Jet Center, and they do a lot of leg-kicking training. They hit their shins against the heavy bag, and they just bang away. Now, sure, beating on the heavy bag toughens up your shins and your feet, but it also deadens the nerves. It closes off the blood flow to that area, so later in life you're going to have very poor circulation in your lower leg. Pretty soon you'll notice that your toes are always cold.

The same thing happens when you practice toughening your body. The dumbest thing I ever saw anybody do was take blows to the body—he just stood there and let a guy punch him in the stomach. Every time you take hard contact like that, you bleed. You have hundreds of thousands of cells in your stomach wall, and every time you bruise one of those cells, it dies. Eventually, you lose the ability to regenerate, and you can have permanent damage.

I'm not saying that muay Thai training will permanently injure you, but when you train your body to become a weapon, you change its molecular structure. You change the cells themselves. Something has to give, and sometimes it can be permanent.

I don't think muay Thai is the art of the 1990s. It's what people think is neat right now. People are interested in the training aspect of it, and it works well for self-defense. In a self-defense situation, if I'm out there fighting a guy on the street, I'm not going to kick to the face. I've probably got jeans on, so I can't reach that high. Also, on the street, if I slip and fall, there's no referee to say, "Time out!" I'm going to get stomped on. So leg kicks in a self-defense situation are great. You'd be surprised by what a side kick to the knee or a roundhouse to the back of the leg will do, especially if you've got a pair of hard shoes on. If you hit your opponent's quadriceps with the toe of your shoe, the fight will be over pretty quick.

I understand people's interest in muay Thai training, because the train-

ing produces the toughest fighters I've ever seen. They scare me. They don't know what pain is. You put any boxer in the ring with a Thai stylist, and he wouldn't last a round. When Rick Roufus fought a Thai boxer recently in Las Vegas, he broke the Thai boxer's jaw. But the guy came back and beat the hell out of Rick. They're tough, but their careers often last only three or four years, and that's after training since age 5! What good is it if your career only lasts that long?

THE TOP 10 KARATE FIGHTERS OF ALL TIME

June 1990

In the early 1980s, I was asked by a magazine to list my top 10 karate fighters. No. 1 was Joe Lewis. I picked Joe because I've never met anybody who said they enjoyed sparring with Joe Lewis. I sparred him several times and I learned a lot, but I didn't enjoy it—it hurts! Joe is very strong, very powerful, very quick, and he knows where to hit you. Joe, in my estimation, was probably the best because he was always in great physical condition, he was strong, powerful, he didn't mind getting hit, and he liked to hit you.

My second choice was Chuck Norris. When I first started practicing karate in 1966, Norris was the epitome of the karate man. When I saw him on television doing jump spinning back kicks and different combinations, he became my hero. I saw him fight several times, and if he's not No. 1, he's definitely No. 2.

Mike Stone was my third choice. I never saw Mike fight; I'm just going by what other people have told me. Mike was mean, he was very aggressive, and the word "lose" wasn't in his vocabulary. His attitude was, "If we're going to fight, we're going to fight hard." His fights weren't pretty, from what I understand, but he was a winner. And when he beat you, you knew he won.

My fourth choice was Ron Marchini. I fought Ron in 1970. He was a very good counterpuncher, good technician and good all-around karate fighter. In 1969, he was voted top competitor on the mainland team in the Mainland vs. Hawaii series, and he deserved that honor. Ron was a superb fighter.

My fifth choice was Tonny Tulleners. I never saw him fight, but I met him about four years ago. He's a tall, rough-and-tumble guy. I watched him spar with his students, if that's what you want to call it—he beat on them. He had a fantastic reverse punch, great timing, great distancing and good movement—he made me believe everything I'd heard. Tonny was one of the best ever.

Sixth, I had Skipper Mullins. I fought Skipper once in Dallas. That was enough. I won that fight, but Skipper was the one I fashioned my kicks after. He was the first one I'd seen throw a roundhouse kick with the forward leg and be effective with it. I modeled my kicking after that.

Next on my list was Mike Warren. Mike was one of the best fighters the United States has ever produced. He had all the agility in the world, all the speed and all the confidence. At one Battle of Atlanta, he beat everybody. He beat me, he beat Darnell Garcia, he beat a bunch of guys. He was a superb athlete and a phenomenal kicker. We fought four times, and he won twice and I won twice. Unfortunately, Mike was hampered by politics; he was a Korean stylist and his instructors didn't want him to fight in tournaments outside the Korean system.

Frank Smith, No. 8 on my list, had the same problem. I've never seen Frank fight, but from what a lot of respected fighters tell me, Frank is one bad dude—a great technician and strong fighter. But, again, politics came into the picture. Frank and Tonny rarely fought in open tournaments. Warren, Tulleners and Smith didn't get the credit and recognition they deserved.

No. 9 was Howard Jackson. Howard and I have sparred, and we became very good friends. Howard is a superb technician—greased lightning, very fast. His career was cut short by a knee injury. Can you imagine being

Joe Lewis vs. Chuck Norris

the No. 1 fighter in the entire country, being at the top of your career and walking into a ring to fight at a small tournament in Denver, slipping on a cup, and tearing up your knee? That's exactly what happened to Howard, and it ruined his career—a real shame.

Last on my list of greats was me. I don't know why I should be listed here, except that I guess I was very lucky. I like to kick, and I like to fight. I guess I enjoy that one-on-one confrontation. Every time I fought, I never thought about losing. I feel the way Mike Stone does: If we're going to spar, let's spar. But if we're calling points, then there's going to be a winner and a loser—and I'm going to be the winner.

There are some guys I had to leave off the list. I think that Anthony "Mafia" Holloway and Kevin Thompson are probably two of the best fighters around today. And another guy who should definitely be listed is Benny "The Jet" Urquidez because Benny was a superb point fighter before he got into full-contact karate. He was and still is one of the best because he's willing to fight under *any* rules.

I look over this list and I see something in common. There are six of us here—Joe Lewis, Chuck Norris, Mike Stone, Tonny Tulleners, Frank Smith and myself—who hated to lose. I remember losing at point tournaments, and people would invite me to the post-tournament party.

I'd say, "*Bleep* you! I ain't going to no *bleeping* party! I'm pissed!" I'm a perfectionist. I want to win every time. And I want every technique I throw to score. If I beat you 15-1 and still missed three or four kicks, I'm upset. I want to be perfect. The guys I picked on this list were like that.

SPARRING THE EX-CHAMP

September 1990

For years I've traveled around the world, teaching martial arts seminars. At the end of each seminar, I always offer to spar anybody in attendance so I can work individually with the people and give them a chance to see my legwork. When I spar, I kick probably 99 percent of the time, so they can see the leg in action and find out firsthand how it all works.

I really enjoy this part of the seminar because I like to spar. I like to spar little kids, I like to spar women, I like to spar guys, and the bigger and better they are, the more I like it. The more they work with me, the more I like to work with them. No points are called—the whole idea is to go out and experiment, try your ideas against mine. They hit me, which helps them, and I hit them, which shows them that what I teach really works.

I have nothing to prove anymore, and I don't want to go home with a black eye or a busted rib.

But before we start sparring, I always tell them, "I will go as hard as you go. If anybody wants to go really hard, wants to do some kickboxing, fine. Tell me now. We'll sit everybody down, and we can kickbox for a couple of minutes so everybody can watch it." So far, no one has taken me up on that offer.

But you know what? I've never taught a seminar without at least one person trying to nail me while we spar, and I mean *nail* me. You can see it in their eyes. It's one of those things where you're sparring and just tippy-tapping around, and suddenly here comes this Sunday haymaker left hook or a spinning backfist.

I remember sparring this kid in upstate New York, and he said, "Please, let's just go easy, Mr. Wallace."

And I said, "Fine, I'll play as hard as you want."

So we go out there and I tap him on the side of the face with a couple of hook kicks, and every time I ask him if he's OK, and he says, "Yeah."

Then, all of a sudden he starts throwing these real hard spinning back kicks. He starts hitting me on the arms, knocking me back. So I think, "OK, he's upped the ante," and I hit him hard once, and he quits. I say, "Let's go another round," and he says, "Oh, no thanks, Mr. Wallace."

These guys are not problems, really. Usually I can pick them out quickly, and then I just cut the matches short. If we're sparring and I can see him winding up, I'll let him throw a couple of them, then I'll say, "OK, break, change partners," just to keep him from hurting me. If he starts hitting me real hard, I'll hit back harder, just to keep him off me. I'm 45; I'm going to survive. I have nothing to prove anymore, and I don't want to go home with a black eye or a busted rib.

Now, Troy Worth of Leucadia, California, has written a letter saying I gave him a mild concussion while sparring at a seminar (*Black Belt* Letters, July 1990). I really wish he'd mentioned where and when the seminar was, what I did at it and so forth, because I frankly don't remember the incident.

If I nailed Troy, there are two possible reasons why: No. 1, it was an accident. If so, I apologize. When I spar at my seminars, my goal is to kick the opponent in the head. Usually I use speed, not power, but I set the opponent up. If I fake a roundhouse kick, the opponent tends to move his head out of its way right into a hook kick, and vice versa. Troy says I hit him in the head with a hook kick. Did he maybe *run into it*? If so, I apologize.

The other possible reason I nailed Troy is that he was coming in awfully strong at me. If so, I don't apologize. I don't mind getting hit, but when you spar me, it's supposed to be a learning situation; it's not to see if you can beat up Bill Wallace. It's to try the techniques, and it needs an attitude of mutual respect. Like I said earlier, when you try to hit me hard, I will survive. I'll hit you back a little bit harder simply to keep you off me because I don't want to get hurt. I just don't heal like I used to heal.

ED PARKER:
SPORT KARATE WILL MISS HIM THE MOST

May 1991

When *kenpo* karate master Ed Parker died on December 15, 1991, it was a great blow to the sport as well as to the art of karate. I met Mr. Parker in 1967, when my instructor introduced me to him at his school in Pasadena, California. He seemed like a very nice gentleman. Jim Harrison and Mike Stone were also there, and I met all these people—my idols, you might say. Being a star or a person with his kind of martial arts background, he could have been kind of snooty or whatever.

In 1969, Mr. Parker invited me to fight at a tournament in Hawaii. It was the mainland versus the Hawaii team. I was part of the mainland team with Ron Marchini and several others.

Also in 1969 (which was a very good year for me as far as competition goes), I was afforded the chance to compete at the Salt Lake City World Championships. Luckily, I won that tournament. Steve Sanders and I were supposed to fight for the grand championship, but he had to go back to Los Angeles for some reason, and they declared me the champion. It would have been a good match. Steve beat me earlier that day. It was double elimination, and I was looking forward to fighting him again in the finals.

Mr. Parker was absolutely fantastic as far as competition goes. He had a very open mind. Because I'm primarily a high kicker, he didn't dissuade me from throwing kicks to the head. He didn't say, "Don't do this," or, "Don't do that because you're not going to get a point."

He just said, "Work it in with your other techniques, but make sure that if they don't call your kick, you can come back with something else. You have to be able to modify. You have to be able to change. If they're not calling techniques, you have to be able to throw something they do call." His advice has stayed with me for a long, long time.

Everybody knows about Ed Parker's International Karate Championships. They were held every August in Long Beach, California. I think, with the demise of Mr. Parker, somebody needs to take hold and run that event because it's a great tournament. I'd hate to see it fall by the wayside.

Mr. Parker had a very big influence on the sport of karate. I remember when I first came to California in 1967 to watch the Internationals. At the black belt meeting, they decided to seed Joe Lewis and Chuck Norris, because Joe had just won a big tournament in New York and Chuck had won a big tournament somewhere else.

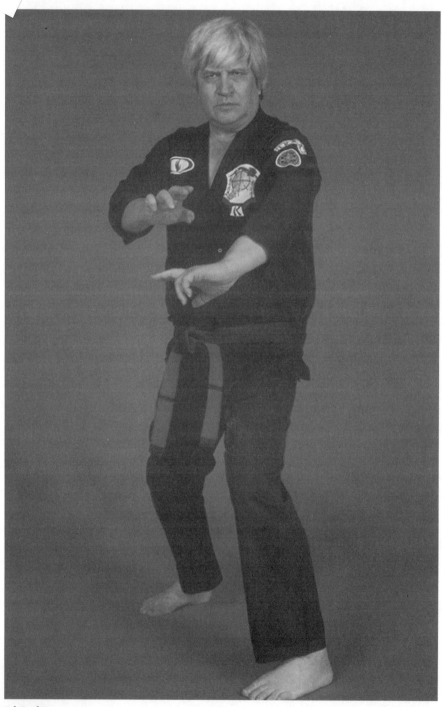

Ed Parker

Mr. Parker said, "OK, you guys are going to be seeded into the finals."
Somebody said, "But I came to this tournament to have the chance to fight Mr. Lewis or Mr. Norris. I don't want to have them seeded." When Joe was fighting, people wanted to see how they could do against his backfist or his side kick—they wanted to see if they could get out of the way of it or not. When Chuck was fighting, people wanted to see if they could get out of the way of his spinning back kick or his rear-leg roundhouse kick, or some really good sneaky movement that Chuck had.

So Mr. Parker stood up and said, "Well, if it's all right with Mr. Norris and Mr. Lewis, and if it's OK with anybody else who might be seeded (referring to Skipper Mullins), all the black belts have to fight all the way through."

As I watched this meeting, I thought, "Wow, here's a man who, even though he's really high up as far as influence goes, is still down to earth because he understands what the competitors want." The competitors like to fight. They want their chance at those guys. And everybody fought. Chuck fought all the way through. Joe fought all the way through. Skipper fought all the way through. It was great.

Ed Parker was a very nice gentleman. He gave me the chance to go to Hawaii to fight. He gave me the chance to go to Salt Lake City and fight for the world championship. He was a guest at many seminars I've given, and he was a really fantastic person as far as I'm concerned. I don't know of anyone who ever said anything bad about Mr. Parker. He did so much for the sport aspect of karate, and I think I speak for everybody in the martial arts world when I say I'm going to miss him.

WHAT'S KEEPING THE MARTIAL ARTS OUT OF THE OLYMPICS?

December 1992

I have a problem with *taekwondo* being in the last two Summer Olympics. Don't get me wrong, taekwondo is a very nice sport; it's fun to watch, the competitors do a lot of kicking and a lot of spinning and so forth. I'm definitely interested in that type of fighting. But here's my problem: It's totally unrealistic as far as fighting goes. Taekwondo is supposed to be fighting.

I'm a kicker—that's what I'm known for. But I can't understand why Olympic taekwondo rules would allow me to kick a guy in the head as hard as I can but not allow me to punch him in the face. The only punches you can use in Olympic-style taekwondo are straight punches to the padded area of the body.

Furthermore, sweeps are not allowed in Olympic taekwondo, nor are grabbing techniques. In fact, the competitors don't even use fighting stances—their hands are down and they are constantly switching their forward legs. They're not even worried about getting punched in the face—all they're worried about is the kicking. Even when they do get within punching range, they push each other away rather than move in and work combinations. If you put a boxer in the ring against a taekwondo guy, the minute the boxer gets in close, the fight is going to be over because the boxer's left hook or uppercut is going to knock the taekwondo guy out.

If you're going to have an Olympic sport, all you really need is a uniform set of rules.

If you're going to have martial arts in the Olympic Games, you're going to have to include taekwondo, karate, kickboxing, etc. You can't have taekwondo in the Olympics and not have karate. Olympic boating has one-man rowing and two-man rowing, and they have separate events for kayaking. Olympic wrestling includes divisions for both Greco-Roman and freestyle wrestling. Olympic fencing has three divisions: sabre, épée and foil. So why not have separate divisions for martial arts?

I would love to see karate in the Olympics, but I honestly don't believe karate would be a big spectator sport, for the same reason taekwondo isn't a spectator sport. If tournament karate was like it appears in the film *The*

Karate Kid, it would be very exciting to watch. But it's not. In real life, you often can't tell one point from another.

What people have to realize is that (and I'm sure I'm going to get letters about this), if we want to have a viable sport, we have to have spectators. We have to change the rules somehow so the spectators will enjoy what they are seeing. Volleyball used to have the same problem the martial arts have now. When I was at Ball State, even though we had the second- or third-ranked volleyball team in the country, we only had about 50 spectators at each match because of the way the game was played. But now they use jump serves, and players run across the court to spike; they've changed the rules a little to make it more exciting.

We have fantastic athletes in kickboxing, men like Pete Cunningham and Rick Roufus. They're really sharp and really tough. They can do all the things you see Steven Seagal and Jean-Claude Van Damme do in the movies—but they do it for real. But does it matter if nobody's watching?

I would have loved to represent the United States if karate had been in the Olympics when I was competing. It would have been great. I'm too old to compete now, but I'd still love to coach if karate ever becomes an Olympic event.

And why can't we have Olympic kickboxing? Every major country in the world has kickboxing now. There are kickboxers in Russia, Germany, Argentina and Asia, and they're all really good. You still have to worry about whether or not to allow leg kicks, knees and elbows, but if you're going to have an Olympic sport, all you really need is a uniform set of rules.

If martial arts are going to be successful in entering the Olympic Games, they need to constitute one broad category, with many smaller divisions within that category, like karate, taekwondo and kung fu. And I'd like to see kickboxing as one of those smaller divisions. Kickboxing is as good a choice for an Olympic sport as yachting or synchronized swimming, isn't it?

THE BRUCE LEE MYSTIQUE
April 1993

When you mention Bruce Lee, the word that comes to my mind is "legend." He had superb technique, an enormous amount of power and speed, and graceful, fluid movements. His movie fight scenes were flashy, choreographed very well and almost beautiful to watch, like a dance.

Unfortunately, I never met him. When he was popular in the 1960s and early 70s, I was living in Indiana and Tennessee and didn't travel to California when he was there. I started fighting in 1967, but I was a young guy out chasing girls, working out, playing football and wrestling. Therefore, I didn't know much about Lee at the time. All I knew was that he was the guy who beat people up and kicked them in the head in the movies. I thought that was neat.

If I *had* met him, I probably would have stepped on my tongue. I wish I could have worked out with him. I was fairly innovative with my kicking techniques and my combinations, but it would have been a godsend to get his ideas, compare notes and discuss techniques. I would have loved to swap tales with him.

Lee died at the peak of his career, leaving behind only speculation about the paths his life and career would have taken and a legacy that will never perish.

I have several friends who knew Lee. They said he was responsive to questions. He worked out with them and exchanged ideas. Based on my conversations with Chuck Norris, Bob Wall, Joe Lewis, and Bruce Lee's wife Linda, he was a very intelligent fighter and had the super ability to adapt to changing situations. He also had a great sense of perfecting movement, which is what the martial arts are all about. For example, Lee had the ability to block an attack in a way that left his attacker vulnerable to a counterattack. Lee's strong points were his superb technique, speed and power. I don't think he had any weak points.

Lee's talents appealed to me for the same reason they appealed to everyone else. It was almost mystical to have this small guy beat up guys who were 6 feet 3 inches tall and 240 pounds. They attacked him, and suddenly they were on their backs. The American people thought this was great because he was doing something they couldn't do, which is why we go to movies and sporting events; people want to see somebody do something they can't. Lee could do it all, especially fight.

The martial arts films from the 1960s and '70s, especially *Enter the Dragon* and *Fists of Fury*, are a little funny compared to today's martial arts movies, particularly the fight scenes and dialogue. Although the fight scenes were very well-choreographed, they were different from today's. In Lee's movies, one person at a time would attack him, he'd beat him up, another guy would attack him, he'd beat him up, etc. There was very little blood, by today's standards.

He brought a lot of boxing into play, as well. My good friend Bob Wall said Lee never sparred and never knew how to fight. I am not saying Wall is wrong, but for someone who supposedly never sparred, Lee had very conceptual ideas about why something would work or not.

Lee's impact on the martial arts has lasted because he was the first big star. He's now a legend who, like James Dean, died at the peak of his career, leaving behind only speculation about the paths his life and career would have taken and a legacy that will never perish. As long as there are martial arts in America, people will remember Bruce Lee.

THE CRIME FIGHTER

September 1993

I've been doing martial arts seminars in Florida for the Guardian Angels for five or six years. Awhile back, they asked me to go on a patrol with them, and I said, "Sure." I'd never done anything like that, but I'm for anything that might make the crime rate go down.

We started at midnight, and we were out for about three hours. The first thing we did was patrol an area that is apparently known for its prevalence of drugs. There were eight people in our patrol, and we walked in single file. One Guardian Angel walked about 15 or 20 paces in front of us, another walked to one side, and one walked about 15 or 20 paces behind us. We patrolled on foot for about 90 minutes and didn't encounter any problems.

Afterward, we got in a truck and drove to a different area. There were two guys in the front seat of the truck, and the rest of us were in the back. The truck had wire mesh around it, and I asked what it was for. They told me, "You'll see."

Guardian Angels founder Curtis Sliwa (left)

While we were driving, I noticed some people looking at us as if they didn't like us, and I started getting nervous. Despite the Guardian Angels' well-meaning efforts to fight crime, there are many people who don't appreciate what they do; some even call them vigilantes. Suddenly, a bunch of bricks and boards came flying over fences from nearby yards, smashing into the truck. All we could do was keep driving and warn each other to duck as the objects approached. Thankfully, there was no gunfire. No one got hurt, but the truck got beat up.

I support the Guardian Angels 100 percent. First of all, if their patrols reduce the crime rate, then I'm all for it. Second, they're unarmed. All they do is look for illegal activity, such as assaults, rapes, robberies, car thefts or people selling drugs. They don't shoot people, beat them up or pick on anybody. They're just conspicuous. If they think someone committed a crime, they detain the suspect. Basically, they just make their presence felt, which often can be enough to force a thief, rapist or drug dealer to go someplace else.

Another reason I support the Guardian Angels is that I don't think there are enough police to handle all of the crime today. Most of the police seem to support the Guardian Angels. While we were on patrol, a lot of police officers came up to us and said things like, "Keep up the good work," and, "Thanks for the help."

It was quite an experience going on patrol with the Guardian Angels; it was fun and enjoyable. I respected them beforehand, but my respect definitely increased after that night. Except for a T-shirt, a beret and the self-satisfaction they get from helping the community, they aren't rewarded. My hat goes off to them. I think they are doing a good job.

The Guardian Angels are a group of people who feel like something needs to be done about crime in today's society, and they're willing to give their time, if not their lives, to make a difference. Heck, Guardian Angels founder Curtis Sliwa takes his life in his hands every time he walks out the door.

Are the Guardian Angels successful? I don't know. It's certainly unfortunate that there aren't more of them. This is a group of people trying to better the community by saving lives and cutting the crime rate. And if I had the chance, I would certainly go on patrol with them again.

RINGSIDE AT THE
ULTIMATE FIGHTING CHAMPIONSHIP
March 1994

I was a commentator for the Ultimate Fighting Championship in Denver last November, and basically what the tournament proved is that 95 percent of the fighters out there today do not know how to fight on the ground. If you take a karate fighter or a kickboxer to the ground, you're taking him out of his element and all his power, speed and strength is nullified.

When you say a tournament like this is going to be "anything goes," the fighters think they can use elbows, knees, head butts and hair-pulling, which, theoretically, they could. What they don't understand is that if they're taken to the ground, they can't kick or punch effectively. They might be able to kick a little bit, but it's not going to do any damage.

It's important to know how to fight on the ground because 90 percent of street fights end up there. The guy on the bottom is hurting in a basic street fight because he's going to get pummeled, kicked, kneed and everything else. Usually, only a *jujutsu* or judo player wants to be on the bottom because he can apply choke holds and armbars.

The rules at the Ultimate Fighting Championship were definitely slanted toward jujutsu players. Competitors couldn't wear boxing gloves or wrap their hands, but the jujutsu guy, Royce Gracie, was allowed to wear his *gi* and his belt. What people don't understand is that jujutsu players know how to take their gi top and use it as a choking device; it's like another hand. It could be a disadvantage also, but who knew how to capitalize on it? Nobody knew any mat work, so the jujutsu player was very effective. Karate people don't practice mat work, and *taekwondo* people have no idea what mat work even is. Mat work takes endurance, strength, movement and a lot of sweat. That's why a lot of people who take judo don't want to do the mat part of training—they'd rather just stand up and throw each other around and look cool. But mat work is very important.

I don't like this no-holds-barred kind of fighting at all; it's too bloody, and the human body can withstand only a certain amount of punishment. When you have bone striking against bone, something has to give. I like to watch good technique. I like to watch someone beat somebody with skill, not brute force. So I didn't enjoy watching this tournament, except for Gracie. He went out there and said, "You guys can do whatever you want to do to me, and I'm still going to beat you." He won all of his matches in 90 seconds or less, and he did what members of the Gracie family have been saying for years: They can take you down, they can beat you, they can choke you out, and nobody can hit them.

I wondered why the other fighters didn't prepare for this kind of fight. The thing is that, of the three fighters Gracie fought, not one of them threw a punch, and not one of them threw a kick. Not one! During the telecast, I was saying, "Why isn't he punching? Why isn't he kicking? At least make it look good. At least keep Royce off balance somehow." The other fighters were either very ill-prepared, or Gracie was very good at taking them down.

Some people have suggested that the fights were set up to make the Gracie family look good, but the other fighters weren't nobodies. *Kenpo* stylist Zane Frazier is a very good fighter. Kickboxer Kevin Rosier, even though he'd been retired and weighed over 300 pounds, was still able to fight. *Savate* stylist Gerard Gordeau is 38, but he was still in good condition. Pat Smith, a two-time winner of the bare-knuckle Sabaki Challenge tournament, was very, very tough. It's not that these fighters weren't the best of their styles; they were probably the only ones who volunteered to compete at the event. If they'd asked me to fight in the tournament, I would have said, "No, thank you."

And the Ultimate Fighting Championship *was* a no-holds-barred tournament, regardless of the criticism. *Sumo* wrestler Teila Tuli didn't just receive a bloody nose; he had three teeth knocked out, a broken nose, a broken jaw and a broken cheekbone. The guy who did that to Tuli, Gerard Gordeau, broke his own hand and foot from the two shots he delivered to hurt the sumo wrestler.

The only things the fighters weren't allowed to do was kick to the groin or use their fingers in the opponent's eyeballs. I understand the rule regarding eye shots, because you want to be able to see when the tournament is over, but I don't see why they didn't allow groin kicks. If you allow knees, elbow strikes, full-power punches to the face and everything else to the body, why not techniques to the groin? I thought it should have been a legal target, and I would like to see some changes. I also thought the fighters should have been able to wear whatever they wanted, other than padding on the arms or legs. If the kickboxer wanted to wear boxing gloves, he should have been allowed to, because that's what he's used to training with.

WILL FIGHT FOR JUNK FOOD

September 1994

I believe it's important to take good care of your body and put the right substances in it. In order to keep up your energy level, you have to give your body good fuel. But I have a fantastic metabolism, and I think my body operates best on junk food.

I pretty much live on chicken strips, hamburgers, french fries and ice cream. I haven't changed my diet since high school, not even when I was fighting full-contact karate professionally. And I haven't gained a pound. Since I've retired from full-contact karate, I've actually *lost* half a pound.

Although I wouldn't recommend my diet for others, junk food doesn't slow me down at all. My metabolism is good enough now that I can stop and eat on the way to the gym and immediately start my workout. In fact, two hours before my retirement fight against Robert Biggs, I had a Wendy's

plain triple-decker hamburger, a large order of french fries, a large Coke and, for dessert, I had a large milkshake. I felt so good. I figured, if Biggs hits me, I'll just throw up on him.

You have to realize that it's important for me to stay flexible. I have to have lubrication in the joints because I like to do a lot of kicking. So I eat lots of greasy hamburgers and french fries to get that lubrication. You'll notice that when I kick, you don't hear any squeaking. And the knee works real good because of all that oil.

Seriously though, I think it's absolutely stupid that I eat all that stuff. I don't know why this diet works so well for me, but it does. I eat junk food all the time, and the worse it is, the better it tastes. But I also eat a lot of fruit, which seems to balance it out and provides me with vitamins and minerals.

I also work out regularly. But after years of hard training as a professional kickboxer, my training now is basically fun. When I was fighting professionally, training was a job. And as most professional fighters will tell you, it's an outright hard job because you have to do it every day, whether you feel like it or not.

After I retired, training became fun. I try to do five to eight three-minute rounds on the heavy bag. If I get tired, I just stop. Then I do two or three minutes of shadowboxing to loosen up my shoulders and arms, and then three or four three-minute rounds of jumping rope. After I've got my heart pumping real well, I'll stretch for a couple minutes, then go over to the horizontal bar and do slow kicks to strengthen my muscles and tendons. I also practice slow movements to work on my fighting techniques and make sure I'm doing them correctly. Then I'll do five rounds of what I call "shadowkicking," which is like shadowboxing, except you're using your legs. After that, I rest for a little while and then do my sit-ups, pull-ups, dips and push-ups for the upper body. I do this three or four times a week. I'd do it every day if I could, but my golf game gets in the way.

LIVING THE BLACK BELT LIE

October 1994

I believe the way the belt-ranking system is now, they should just disregard it entirely. When I first started training in karate, there were only four belts: white, green, brown and black. Now there are many different colors, because everyone wants to prove they're better than the next guy by having a different belt. Some people justify it by saying that it helps motivate kids, but I think it all just comes down to ego.

It's gotten to the point where, if a student trains for two weeks longer than someone else, he wants to prove his superiority by having a different color belt. A black belt used to mean you were the best; now it doesn't mean anything. I've been involved in martial arts for 30 years, and according to my instructor, I'm a third-degree black belt. But rank is not important to me because I don't have a school. Still, I don't understand why there are people younger than me walking around wearing the red-and-white striped belts of a master or, better yet, a guy who's a 10th-degree black belt who is supposedly a grandmaster yet has less experience in the martial arts than I do.

I always thought that, when you became a master, it meant you did every technique perfectly, like you were walking on water. But I don't see that many people out there walking on water. I think we've glorified the ranking system to the point where, when someone gets a black belt, he automatically thinks he's learned everything. That's just not true.

One thing that upsets me more than anything is when you have these prepubescent kids who are first-, second- or third-degree black belts, but who don't understand the application of the techniques they're performing. They might be able to do them well, but they have no idea *why* they're doing them.

A black belt is just like a college degree or a high-school diploma. Once you get a black belt, your job is to instruct other people. To do this, you must be able to explain the techniques, not just say, "I can do a side kick better than you can, so I should be a black belt." I've seen some fantastic people out there who can't kick very well at all. I've seen some fantastic instructors and fantastic fighters who have terrible, sloppy technique, but they know what their bodies can do, and they know how to be effective.

I'm sure money has something to do with the loss of integrity in the belt-ranking system. If I had a karate school, my job would be to keep students in that school. Now let's say you are 8 years old and have been practicing karate for three years. If I don't let you test for a black belt because I don't think you're ready, you'll just quit and go somewhere else. I see this happening all the time. The kids want to be glorified and think they're tough. And I guess wearing that black belt gives them the confidence they're lacking.

A black belt used to mean you were the best; now it doesn't mean anything.

Personally, I can do just as well without a belt as with one. But for some people, a belt is the first thing they have to put on. Why? To prove themselves? When I'm working out, I don't even wear a belt. I can walk into a karate school wearing a pair of sweat pants and work out, and everybody there is going to know I'm a black belt just by the way I perform. I've never had to prove to anyone that I've earned my rank.

LIFE ON THE SEMINAR CIRCUIT

October 1995

Joe Lewis, Dan Inosanto, Michael DePasquale and I conduct martial arts seminars all over the world. Usually, the people hosting the seminar will fly us in, we do the seminar and hopefully our presence helps build their school's reputation and enrollment.

We do these seminars in good faith. Most of the hosts want to wait until after the seminar to pay us because they expect our fees will be generated by the seminar. This usually isn't a problem, as far as I'm concerned. On occasion, the host will call me and say, "Fifty to 60 people are expected to attend the seminar."

My response is always, "What happens if only 10 come? Am I still going to get paid the same amount of money?"

Not long ago, I did a seminar for some people in Florida. I had promised them two days. On the first night of the event, only four paying guests were there. The next day, three people showed up. I've done seminars with over 600 in attendance, and I've also done them for an audience of 15. But this was the first time only three people showed up. This particular time, I settled for my expenses and a small fee.

You'd be surprised how many martial artists don't think it's a problem to screw you over just because they work in the same field.

Afterward, I asked how they had advertised the seminar. The host said he'd sent fliers about a month before the event. I asked him, "Did you follow up with anything?" and he said he hadn't attempted to call anyone or follow up in any way.

Karate people are kind of silly in that regard. For the most part, we're not business people. If we hired Bruce Lee for a seminar, we'd probably just tell our friends and fellow martial artists and expect them all to show up. We tend to think that if we tell one person, he'll tell everyone else, and 1,500 people will show up at the seminar. But it doesn't work like that. If I tell one friend, and he forgets about it, the invitations end there. Bruce Lee would show up and perform in front of an empty room.

About seven years ago, I did an exhibition match with boxer Thomas Hearns in Miami. The promoters gave me a check that bounced. At least Tommy's check bounced, too, so I don't feel as bad.

You'd think that people would worry about their reputations. I've done work for some very prominent karate people who never paid me. About 15 years ago, I did a seminar for one of the top fighters in the United States, and my check bounced. There had been 35 or 40 people in attendance, which made me wonder where the money had gone.

About a year ago, I did a seminar for a guy in Philadelphia. I didn't want to do it because I was about to go to Germany for a month, but he begged and pleaded with me to do it, and he offered to pay me more. Finally, I said I would do it for the regular price, but I had to leave immediately after the seminar. So I did the seminar, and the check bounced. He promised to send another check, but nothing ever arrived. When I called him, he said he would send me two money orders. Still nothing arrived. I called again, and he said he was having financial problems. But there were 100 people at his seminar!

Later, when I heard he'd held a tournament with 450 competitors that brought in $15,000, I called him. I asked him if he could send me my money, and he said someone had stolen it.

I don't threaten people. But you'd be surprised how many martial artists don't think it's a problem to screw you over just because they work in the same field. Joe Lewis sometimes gets a bad check, but Joe is bigger than I am, and he'll grab the guy by the ears, put him against a wall and say, "I want my money." So they pay him.

If the host is having financial problems, he should let us know. We're all flexible in that respect, because this is how we make a living. If the host doesn't have a good experience, he's not going to invite me back. My job is to make sure he's pleased with the seminar, and I expect to get paid for it.

HOW PREVALENT ARE DRUGS IN THE MARTIAL ARTS?

January 1997

I've never seen or heard much in the way of drug use in the martial arts world. However, because of my association with Elvis Presley and John Belushi, people often ask me about my thoughts on the subject.

I met Belushi at a New Year's Eve party in 1980. He invited me to go on tour with him, and we worked out every day I was with him. Although he was a heavy person, he could run a mile, do three sets of 50 sit-ups, and then do three sets of 10 bench presses at about 120 pounds. I don't know too many obese people his size who could do the things he could do.

Belushi liked to eat, and he drank a little. When I was working with him, we'd go to parties sometimes. People would come up and shake my hand, and I'd pull away with two or three vials of cocaine in my hand. They'd say, "This is for John. Tell him I'm available if there are any film projects coming up." I'd flush the stuff down the toilet.

I remember back in the early 1970s, marijuana was very prevalent, but I don't think that it is now in the martial arts. I know back then there were a few guys using marijuana. After a tournament, some of the competitors might gather in a room and talk about how they'd smoked some pot the night before. Or maybe they'd smoke some after the tournament.

It all comes down to respecting your body and maintaining your health.

Using marijuana while you're competing makes no sense. Marijuana is primarily a downer; it mellows you out. It would be very hard to compete in martial arts while under the influence of marijuana. I wouldn't think competitors would use marijuana, now that we've learned so much more about its negative effects.

There might be steroid use in the martial arts, because some competitors might think using steroids would help them. But performance-enhancing drugs aren't worth the health risk; for one thing, martial arts competitors simply don't make enough money to make it worthwhile to take dangerous drugs.

Alcohol was very prevalent back in my competition days. One of the main purposes for going to a tournament back then was to get together with old friends. You might win a trophy, but you never won any money. You would arrive on a Friday and start partying with the other competitors. After the tournament, it was just one big party. Competitors still party now; they might get a little buzzed or a little happy. But back then, I could name five or six guys who got bombed out of their minds at tournaments.

It all comes down to respecting your body and maintaining your health. We should all be concerned with our health—especially after hearing about all the recent deaths of martial artists at relatively young ages. After training for years and staying in good physical condition, all of a sudden something changes for some martial artists. As they get older, they might not train as often or as hard as they used to. I also believe stress has a lot to do with it. In the martial arts world, there are very few millionaires, so many of us are left wondering where the next paycheck is going to come from.

I'm 51, and not everybody my age continues to train. I worked out for four hours a day when I was competing. But I killed myself for those four hours. Now you talk to guys who claim to work out five or six hours a day, but when you drop by their gym, they're sitting around drinking sodas. And you wonder why they have the gut hanging over their belts. Even though you may want to work out, your priorities change as you get older. When I was in high school and in the service, all I wanted to do was wrestle. Then when I went to college, all I wanted to do was wrestle and practice karate. When I graduated from college, I just wanted to be a fighter. Now things have changed. I'm a little bit older, and I don't want to train as hard. Instead of a four-hour martial arts workout, I'll do one hour of karate and then play three hours of golf.

Unfortunately, it's just too easy when you're older to come up with excuses for not working out. It's OK to say "no" to drugs, as long as you say "yes" to working out and staying in shape.

THE GOLDEN AGE OF MARTIAL ARTS

December 1997

To me, the years 1969 through 1980 constituted the "golden age" of karate. Tournaments became more popular during that time, and the people who competed, like Joe Lewis and Chuck Norris, were known throughout the martial arts world.

One thing that set that era apart is the fact that the competitors didn't wear safety equipment—it was just bare knuckles and bare feet. You had to show expert control, because if you didn't, your opponent would hit you back. I'll be the first to admit that the fighters' technique was not nearly as good then as it is today. Today's fighters use many more weapons. They have more safety padding, so they feel more comfortable throwing a variety of techniques. They can take more chances with the protection they wear.

The competitors in the golden age really had a fighting spirit. We loved to compete, because all we did was fight for trophies; there was no prize money in those days. We felt the purpose of the tournament was for us to get together and have a really good time, not necessarily to win. My favorite part of any tournament was when they called the black belts to prepare to compete; all of us would gather in a corner and start sparring with each other. We would warm up and talk with one another while watching each other spar. That was more fun than the actual competition.

> ## For me, the highlight of the old tournaments was the camaraderie shared by the competitors.

I like to think that the golden-age fighters helped teach today's competitors to throw double- and triple-combination kicks and to kick primarily with their front legs. Although many of the fighters of that era wanted to get inside and punch their opponents, some of us (myself included) liked to keep our distance so we could throw combination kicks and try to set up the punches. We thought that was more artistic.

Perhaps the most noteworthy thing about the golden age of karate was that everybody stayed around to watch the black belts compete. When you go to a tournament today, by the time the black belts fight, everyone is gone. Nobody even cares who wins the grand championship in the black-belt division anymore.

The rules have also changed. Now the sparring is a game of tag. You can't sweep, throw or take your opponent down. Back then, you could do all that. Now, if you touch your opponent, you get a point. If your punch doesn't connect squarely and slides off the opponent, the judges still count it as a point.

Another problem today lies in the scoring of forms competitions: They seem nonsensical and inflated. At a recent tournament I attended, a 12- or 13-year-old kid did a staff form and received three perfect 10 scores. Are you going to tell me that he did a better, stronger, more technical form than a 23-year-old black belt who got scores of 9.5?

Another disappointment is that there are very few post-tournament parties today. There used to be parties after tournaments, at which all the fighters would sit around and talk about the day's competition. We would sit up all night and talk because we hadn't seen each other in months. Now the competitors don't even talk to each other.

For me, the highlight of the old tournaments was the camaraderie shared by the competitors. In those days, it wasn't unusual for nine guys to stay in one hotel room when they went to a tournament. If you couldn't afford a room, someone would find a place for you.

IS KICKING DEAD?

February 1998

In the wake of the continuing downward slide of the sport of kickboxing and the unexpected success of grapplers in events like the Ultimate Fighting Championship, a lot of people are saying that, as a means for competing in full-contact tournaments and even defending oneself on the street, kicking is virtually dead. Following are some insights on the matter from the man who has been called the world's greatest kicker. —Editor

To a certain degree, people are right when they say kicking is dead. To understand this, you have to realize that, if you're going to be a decent kicker, you have to work your legs.

Ever since you came out of your mother's womb, you reached for things with your hands; you don't reach out with your legs. Your legs are used for crawling and then walking, not for picking things up.

You crawl and walk for years and years, then all of a sudden somebody teaches you how to kick a ball, so you learn how to punt, which is basically a front kick. You probably never practice much leg movement to the side, as in a side kick, or much that goes around, as in a roundhouse or hook kick. Your leg just moves to the front because you want to kick a ball.

Then you decide to take up karate so you can learn how to kick. So you go through flexibility exercises that you have never done before. That hurts. You are making the muscles a little stronger, but also a little more tired because you are building up the lactic acid. The muscles are getting bigger, and your leg is much heavier than your arm—and that isn't counting the fact that you don't use it as much or you might be wearing shoes.

If you watch somebody throw a punch at you and just touch your forehead, you'll see that he can do it very quickly. Now watch somebody try to do that with his foot. He has to gauge the distance and possibly move and lean way back to get his leg up there—if he can get it up there at all. Remember that it weighs almost a third of his total body weight.

In kickboxing matches, kicking can be practically nonexistent because fighters find out it's easier to throw a left hook than a jump-spinning back kick. Likewise, it's easier to throw that rear-leg roundhouse kick as hard as possible to the body and look really good than it is to do the jump-spinning back kick.

What happens next? Spectators who are expecting to see fancy kicking techniques don't see any. So why watch kickboxing? They can just go back to boxing, in which the hand techniques are better and the fighters hit each other more often.

The basic realization is that kicking isn't second nature to most people. They have to learn the kicks, then they have to practice them a lot. That often means throwing 15,000 kicks with each leg. In a match, they have to actually tell themselves to kick. And those kicks have to be strong and hard. So they throw five or six of those, then start thinking, "Why should I throw this jump-spinning back kick when I can just throw a rear-leg slamming roundhouse kick to the body and not get nearly as tired?" Endurance is important when they've got to fight 12 rounds and throw a lot of kicks.

Furthermore, martial artists don't believe kicking is as unbeatable as they used to. Part of the reason is that a person needs three things to kick well: balance, flexibility and timing. With punching, you don't have to have any balance; you just step and throw it. The learned movement doesn't have to be there because you've been doing it since you were born.

Kicking is more of an art form. There are some very good kickers out there fighting in point tournaments. They balance on one leg and jump across the floor flicking out kicks with the other leg. A kickboxer would just walk in there and say, "Go ahead, I'm going to take that kick." Then the fancy kicker would fall, and the kickboxer would step on him and beat him to a pulp. When someone kicks like that, he doesn't maintain the balance that a kickboxer has when he throws a power kick.

Is there still an interest among martial artists in kicking? Sure. I just got back from a three-week trip around Europe to conduct seminars. People still want to learn how to kick, how to be flexible, how to place their foot up in the air and hold it there—except they don't want to work at it that hard. They don't want to stretch as hard. They don't want to do the kicking drills. It sounds bad to say it, but it's true.

AMERICANS WORK TO IMPROVE THE MARTIAL ARTS
March 1998

Years ago, nobody could beat the Japanese at judo or the Koreans at taekwondo. *This slowly began to change, however, and even though the two countries are still great at producing athletes who win in their respective sports, Americans can now beat them at their own game. Similarly, a few years ago, Brazilian fighters were defeating everybody in no-holds-barred events like the Ultimate Fighting Championship. Now, American fighters like Maurice Smith, Randy Couture, Don Frye, Mark Kerr and Mark Coleman have learned how to beat the Brazilians at their game. Once again, Americans have proved they can learn how to compete—and win—in any type of competition and under any set of rules.* —Editor

One big difference between American and foreign martial artists is that, if a technique is not in their particular style, foreign martial artists usually won't practice it. This is especially true with traditional martial artists who do taekwondo, *shotokan* karate and other Japanese styles. Americans are different, in that they try to improve their art.

When was the last time you saw a shotokan stylist throw a spinning back kick to the head? For that matter, when was the last time you saw a shotokan stylist throw any type of kick to the head? Things are slowly changing, however: I saw shotokan practitioners in Europe throw spinning back kicks to the head. They probably saw the effectiveness of the technique and decided it could work for them. But because of their adherence to tradition, this would never have happened in the past.

Part of the problem is that most traditional martial arts were created by Asians, who were about 5 feet 4 inches tall. There's no way someone that size is going to fight an American who is 6 feet 2 and be able to kick him in the head. To accommodate themselves, Asians made the rules to fit their particular strengths.

Americans are different because we change the martial art to fit our body type. And because we are generally well-conditioned and fit, we can become successful doing this. As long as we keep an open mind, we can modify an art to make it work even better for us. This is different from the Korean and Japanese approach, in which practitioners often think, "I want to do it just the way I was taught."

A few years ago, I studied a system called *shorin-ryu* karate. I never had to kick above the stomach. Instead, I used front kicks and rear-leg roundhouse kicks to the stomach, and that was it. The first time I sparred with my instructor, I kicked him in the head with a roundhouse kick using my front leg. Immediately after that, he backed up and said, "What did you do?"

I replied, "Sorry, but I saw the opening and I just threw the kick. It felt good."

He responded, "I like that."

I was fortunate enough to have instructors who were open-minded and accepted new techniques whenever they proved successful.

If you watch the most powerful fighters in the world—men such as Maurice Smith or Mike Tyson—you'll see that not every shot they throw knocks somebody out or even makes contact. I've always believed that, contrary to many traditional ways of thinking, if a person possesses speed, he or she can develop a certain amount of power. However, if you have power, you don't necessarily have speed. Most Asian arts teach students to throw the most powerful punch possible, but why throw a powerful punch if you don't hit anything? I'd rather take two or three quick shots and make them add up. This strategy allows you to make contact and thereby force your opponent to worry about the consequences.

Americans are different because we change the martial art to fit our body type.

Everybody is built differently. People have different strengths and weaknesses. Unfortunately, many fighters don't adapt their art to their body. For example, if you're a guy like Sugar Ray Leonard and someone teaches you to fight like Joe Frazier, you'll lose every fight.

Champion kickboxer Joe Lewis is one of my best friends, but there's no way I could fight like he does. He's very strong, fast and tough, and he likes to mix it up. Compared to him, I'm not so strong, but I possess speed. In contrast to Lewis, I don't want to mix it up at all. I don't want you to hit me, period. If there's going to be one hit in the entire match, I want to be the hitter. But we were both successful because we adapted the traditional arts we learned so they better fit our bodies.

ROLE OF PSYCHOLOGY IN MARTIAL ARTS TRAINING

May 1998

Can a student surpass his instructor in their chosen martial art? It's an interesting question. The answer, theoretically speaking, is yes, assuming the student already brings some knowledge and skill to the table. If the teacher does his job and teaches the student everything he knows, the student should become better than the teacher. The new material is added to his experience, theoretically making him better than the instructor.

Unfortunately, this doesn't always happen. There's the instructor's ego to consider. Oftentimes he doesn't want a student to be better than he is because the student's skills could make the instructor look bad in front of the other students.

In many cases, the instructor subconsciously or consciously holds back and doesn't teach the student everything he knows. A lot of instructors tell their students they will never be able to beat them. After repeatedly hearing this, the students eventually begin to believe it.

A related topic involves people who want to be called "master." When it comes to this, I simply don't agree. The only person I would call a master is my father. He's the only one I've ever met that I couldn't beat up. In fact, I generally don't even call people "mister" (one of the few exceptions being the late Robert Trias, and only because he was much older than I and because I had a lot of respect for him).

Many students "know" they can't beat their instructor because of the psychological conditioning they get in class. For example, you might be sparring with your instructor's teacher and beating him to a pulp. You've never seen this opponent before, and you have no preconceived fears or doubts. You couldn't beat your instructor because of the psychology you've developed, but you can beat his teacher. And in some cases, this man could beat your instructor to a pulp.

Psychology is very important in the martial arts. The first time I saw a fight with champion kickboxer Joe Lewis, I was scared to death. He just took guys and beat the tar out of them. Unfortunately, several years later, I had to fight him for a grand championship. Have you ever seen Lewis' knuckles? He's got golf balls in his hands, and keep in mind, this was before people used protective pads. I just hoped that I would last 30 seconds in the ring with him. Lewis was very strong, fast and gifted, and people were afraid to face him—including me.

Since I've fought in many fights, people often ask me if I was afraid right before a match. I answer, "Every time." All it takes is one punch to break something or even kill a person. I'm not a religious person, but if you look at the videotapes of my fights, you'll see me look up into the sky before a fight, hoping to make it out alive.

Oftentimes an instructor doesn't want a student to be better than he is because the student's skills could make him look bad in front of the other students.

Some martial arts instructors yell and scream a lot when they're teaching, and this can make the student better or worse. Sometimes, it can make the student hate his instructor so much that all he can think about is beating him up. However, if a student has been with a certain instructor since he was 15, and now he's 30, he is often hindered psychologically—and scared to death of his instructor.

WEARING A BLACK BELT MEANS BEING RESPONSIBLE, PART 1

October 1998

If you're going to earn a black belt and continue to practice the martial arts, there are certain aspects of the arts and their traditions that you should learn and make an effort to follow. Among them are how to tie your belt, how to bow and how to wear your uniform. There are traditional ways to do each of these things, and there are nontraditional ways. However, being a black belt in any given art carries with it certain expectations.

It's important to learn how to tie your black belt the correct way—that is, the way it was traditionally done. Different arts may have completely different ways of doing this, and that's fine; if you want to break away from your particular tradition and tie your belt any old way you want, you can.

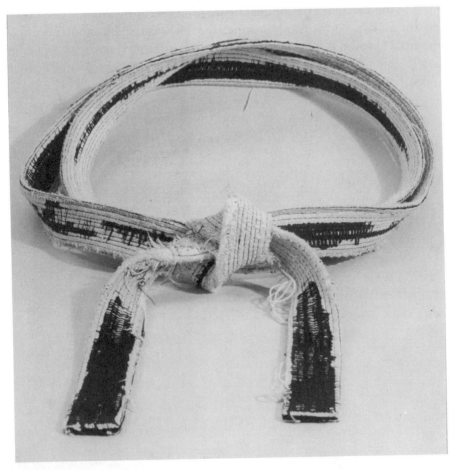

Some people feel a need to be different. But because doing your own thing is not what being part of a traditional martial art is all about, you should not claim to be a practitioner of that art any longer.

Practicing a traditional art means that there's a historical basis for everything you do in the *dojo*. My system is Okinawan *shorin-ryu* karate. We tie the belt in a square knot in which both ends come out of the sides. That was the way it was done in the old days, it was very simple, and that's the way it's still done in that system.

Bowing is the way you recognize the existence of another person according to Asian tradition. It's similar to shaking hands in the Western world. (I've never understood the custom of bowing and shaking hands at the same time, but that's another story.) There are several ways to bow. Some are generic greetings that simply mean "Hello. How are you?" But others, such as the *kenpo* karate bow, are far more complex. As with tying a belt, bowing is taught differently from art to art.

But there will always be people who decide to create their own methods of bowing. But if you practice a traditional martial art—whether it's karate, kung fu, *taekwondo* or something else—your bow should be performed in accordance with what your instructor taught you.

When it comes to wearing a uniform, once again there are certain traditions that should be followed. I've never tucked my *gi* top into my pants, and I never will. It's baggy enough the way it is, and I don't want it to hinder my arm movement. (If I were to fight in a tournament and had my choice, I'd wear a sweat shirt instead of a gi top because with a sweat shirt there's no binding and it's not loose in the arms.) Yet I see a lot of competitors who tuck in their gi tops. It's all right to do this, of course, but if you're just trying to look cool, you should know that it pops right out again after a little bit of activity.

Whether you tie your belt, bow or wear your gi in the traditional way is up to you. But remember that it's important to maintain some uniformity in the martial arts. It's important to understand the traditions behind the customs, just as it is to know the reasons for doing specific hand and foot techniques in a *kata*.

At tournaments and seminars, I hear a lot of spectators say things like, "It doesn't look like karate anymore. It doesn't look like the martial arts anymore." Well, the martial arts community only has itself to blame, as martial artists are the torchbearers of tradition.

WEARING A BLACK BELT MEANS BEING RESPONSIBLE, PART 2

November 1998

There are certain responsibilities a black belt should strive to live up to. Being able to teach, defend himself and show respect at competitions are just a few of them.

A black belt should be able to demonstrate and teach his art effectively. That's part of wearing the rank. He doesn't necessarily need to be a fighter—some people are fighters and some are not. However, he should be able to use his art's techniques in various dangerous situations that may arise.

Pay particular attention to the word "should." Although I was a good competitor, I've never been in a street fight. Therefore, I honestly don't know how I'd fare in one. I don't know for sure how to use my weapons on the street, but I have a pretty good idea. The same should be true of any black belt.

Black belt competition is for a select few, however. If you go into the average karate school, you might find that only about 5 percent of the students have aspirations to compete. And that's fine, because sparring is just one small part of the martial arts. I've only recently come to realize that.

Any black belt interested in competing in tournaments needs to know how to serve as a judge. He needs to know how to distinguish good techniques from bad techniques, and he must understand power, force, flexibility and movement.

Another area in which a black belt should act as a role model involves attitude. Of all the karate schools I've visited, I haven't seen one where the advanced students were disrespectful or annoying. The problem arises only when competition is taking place because many judges' decisions are subjective. Nevertheless, a black belt should always show respect for the judges and the other competitors. Of course, different judges will have different opinions about what constitutes a point. This can cause friction between competitors and officials, but a black belt must remember that it's only a tournament.

In point fighting, it can be more difficult for a black belt to live up to the expectations of his rank. Basically, respect is gone from sparring competition in martial arts tournaments, and while I'm not advocating this, I can understand how it happened: Competitors pay a lot of money and expect to get a fair shake. If he's competing against a big-name fighter and the referee is calling all of the name fighter's points but none of the regular guy's, it can be discouraging. Yet someone who has earned black-belt status should be able to handle the situation.

Before showing disrespect for a judge's decision, a black belt needs to consider the judge's situation. He's doing the best he can. All the yelling and screaming in the world isn't going to change his decision—which he thinks is absolutely correct. Neither is it going to serve any positive purpose.

A black belt should be able to use his art's techniques in various dangerous situations that may arise.

The problem would be eased somewhat if referees could tell competitors why they did or did not score a point for a certain blow. Fighters should not have to wait until the end of their match to ask about the calls that were made. Martial artists have a right to know why certain calls were made and others were not. If the competitor questions a call, most referees will tell him to shut up and wait until after the fight for an explanation. By that time, it will be too late. The responsible black belt will abide by whatever rules are in place.

The challenges of wearing a black belt can be just as great as the challenges of earning one. In the martial arts, the road of progress is never easy.

MARKETING 101

March 1999

If you are a martial artist who is trying to market himself on the seminar circuit, you'll need to pay attention to a few things in order to reach your goals. These include the uniqueness of your material, a friendly personality, merchandising, innovation and a good promoter. I will examine each of these in detail.

First is uniqueness. If you want to succeed on the seminar circuit, you need to offer something unique. If you look at the people out there now, you'll see that they're all experts in some niche of the martial arts. For me, it's kicking and stretching. What some people don't understand is that these people, myself included, are not trying to convert everybody to our art or our way of doing things. What we're doing is presenting ideas. Every champion has something unique to offer the public. If you want to succeed on the seminar circuit, this is a must.

Becoming associated with a product can help get your name circulating within the martial arts world.

The second requirement is personality. One of the reasons I've done well on the seminar circuit is that I like to laugh and joke around with everybody. If you get mad at me, I'll just stick my tongue out, and it will be difficult for you to remain angry. I try to smile a lot, and this has made many people warm up to me. It has always been fairly easy for me to approach people and say, "Hi, I'm Superfoot. How you doing?" And then I stick my leg up in the air because kicking is what I'm known for.

Third is merchandising. Becoming associated with a product can help get your name circulating within the martial arts world. I've recently become involved in the development of a line of sportswear. Going all the way back to my college days, I loved to wear sweat pants and sweat shirts because they're comfortable. Through the years, people have told me that I should start my own line of clothing. A few months ago, my wife Kim and I finally decided to do just that. We wanted to design clothing that was comfortable and of high enough quality to bear the "Superfoot" logo. So we developed some baggy, comfortable sweat shirts and sweat pants that don't bind when you throw a kick or punch.

The fourth requirement is innovation. During my heyday, kickboxing was in its infancy. The sport was new and fresh, and when I came along, there was really nobody out there kicking the way I did. I was the first one to really emphasize that part of the martial arts. I've remained relatively well-known because I was the first to really use kicking as a primary weapon. People still want to learn the way I execute kicks and use them in combinations.

Fifth is promotion. To get an idea of how to do this, take a look at the John Paul Mitchell team. They do an excellent job of promoting their martial artists. Promoter Don Rodrigues knows how to push his athletes, who are phenomenal at what they do. Martial artists often find it hard to talk about themselves, so having a good promoter or publicist can be very valuable.

Publicity in the martial arts has obviously come a long way since my competition days in the late '60s and early '70s. Back then, there was no such thing as self-promotion. The Internet didn't exist, there were no instructional videotapes, and seminars were few and far between. Just about the only way to receive any publicity was through magazines like *Black Belt*. It seems so much easier now for a champion or a great instructor to make a name for himself. It's a shame that more martial artists don't take advantage of all the resources that are available.

HOW MANY WORLDS ARE THERE, ANYWAY?

June 1999

If you ever take a good, hard look at the martial arts tournament circuit, you'll notice that there seems to be a world champion lurking in every corner, every nook and every cranny. A plethora of people claim to be a world champion in their particular fighting style. In addition to often being outright lies, such claims serve only to diminish the credibility of legitimate martial artists who have earned their rank and title the hard way.

In America, the trend of making greater and greater claims about one's competition career has evolved into a ridiculous charade. In martial arts magazines, I read about practitioners who claim to have been world champions in years when no world championship events were held. It would be great if writers could verify the statements made by martial artists, but with so many organizations and tournaments—many of which no longer exist—fact-checking is difficult.

If you want to be called a world champion, you should be willing to fight anybody who steps into the ring.

One of the biggest reasons for this problem is that too many organizations support their own set of world champions. The same thing can be seen—although to a lesser extent—in boxing, where the World Boxing Association, World Boxing Council and International Boxing Federation all sanction their own bouts, crown their own champions and give out their own belts. Each world champion usually refrains from fighting the champions from other organizations because he doesn't want to risk relinquishing what he already possesses. Therefore, the three belts are seldom united in one fighter.

In the martial arts, almost anyone can hold a tournament and call it a world championship. It doesn't matter how good the competitors are, how many people enter or whether the "world" is in any way accurate. A martial artist can win the event and retire the very next day, and he'll be able to claim he's a world champion.

The title of "world champion" should carry much more weight than it does in its current watered-down form. Just how many worlds are there, anyway? Surely there can't be a separate world for every martial artist who claims to be a world champion.

If you want to be called a world champion, you should be willing to fight anybody who steps into the ring. Prove yourself worthy of the title, or stop claiming you're a world champion. It's as simple as that.

As much as having to listen to so many false claims upsets me, it must really tick off the legitimate champions who've retired or are still out there competing. I empathize with people like Benny "The Jet" Urquidez, who became a legitimate world champion and defended his title many times. I won the world championship in 1974 and retired in 1980, and I defended my title 23 times. Does that make me a world champion 23 times over?

The distorted claims of martial artists are also infiltrating the television and movie industries. In an effort to get work, up-and-coming actors tend to exaggerate their martial arts records to impress movie producers. What's to stop those filmmaking executives—who probably don't have a clue about the chaos of the martial arts world—from believing everything they hear? And if an actor does get hired for an action movie, his false claims will be spread even more widely.

Wouldn't it be nice if the martial arts—not just point karate, but also kickboxing, *jujutsu*, full-contact karate, etc.—were run like the World Series? There's no way a baseball team can get away with lying about having won the World Series, because anyone can pick up an almanac and check. When will the martial arts reach that level of organization?

SOLVING THE WORLD-CHAMPION DILEMMA
July 1999

In the June 1999 installment of this column, I talked about the incredible number of illegitimate world champions in the martial arts world and how it not only damages the credibility of those making the claims but also hurts the entire industry. This month, I will offer some potential solutions to this widespread problem that continues to plague the martial arts.

A governing body has to round up the five best fighters in each weight class by recruiting from all the existing associations and organizations, then let them fight to determine the overall winner.

For a brief time during the 1970s, there was some stability in the industry. The Professional Karate Association (PKA) was around then, and it was considered the ultimate competition. For a time, PKA champions were the only world champions. This was great for competitors and for the public. But the situation was ultimately ruined because everybody wanted a piece of the action. Other people wanted to taste success, too, and that led to the formation of many other organizations. The martial arts became like boxing, which boasts more sanctioning bodies than I can count on both hands.

Can all the different factions in the martial arts world be brought together under one roof? While that would certainly be no easy task, one solution might be to create a single governing body to conduct national- and world-championship events. Currently many organizations claim that their winners are world champions, but there needs to be only one, and it must have enough staying power to make itself the only legitimate and universal authority. For example, there is only one Olympic Games. That's why being an Olympic gold medalist carries a lot of weight, while being a martial arts world champion can mean very little.

Exactly how can a governing body determine the true world champions? It has to round up the five best fighters in each weight class by recruiting from all the existing associations and organizations, then let them fight to determine the overall winner.

Lots of people insist that this concept will never work. Strangely enough, these dissenters aren't the fighters; they're the heads of the different karate associations. They don't want their champions to fight the champions of other groups because they already claim to represent the national championship. Why take a chance on losing? The president of one group could lose his reputation in the martial arts world if his fighter lost such a bout.

To the best of my knowledge, the fighters want to fight. If I were one of them, I would want to fight the best to measure my own abilities.

Although I've never been involved in the creation of such an international organization, I would love to be part of such an undertaking. Unlike many people in the martial arts world, I'm bothered when competitors make outlandish, unsubstantiated claims. I hope that everyone who reads this column starts to care, too.

KIDS JUST WANT TO HAVE FUN
November 1999

Teaching the martial arts to 4- and 5-year-old children requires special skills. The key to appealing to that age group is to make sure they have fun in class. In this column, I'll discuss ways to make martial arts training fun, along with other methods for keeping kids interested. I'll also offer recommendations on what to avoid with this age group.

One way to make the martial arts more appealing is to make training into a game. When kids attend my seminars, I sometimes teach them a roundhouse kick and then ask to see how fast they can throw it. Then I might tell them to try to kick my hand before I can move it, or I might create a game in which they see how high they can hold their kicking leg.

Maintaining the children's interest is a lot easier if the instructor enjoys what he does. It's easy to distinguish an instructor who likes kids from one who doesn't: The one who does will probably be seen hugging his young students or giving them high-fives after class. I like to bond with the kids during my children's seminars by sparring with each one and letting everybody kick me in the butt or punch me in the face.

Being around slightly older kids and adults can guide children in the learning process. The younger kids look up to the older kids and dream about being like them someday. If older adults are the only ones around, the youngsters may ask themselves, "Gosh, am I going to be 45 before I can throw a kick like that?" But if they see a 7- or 8-year-old doing it, they become encouraged.

A laid-back and fun martial arts class is always more appealing to kids than a strict karate class. Youngsters will stop going to the strict class, especially if the instructor continually scolds them. Pretty soon, the students' parents will become aware of this and take their business elsewhere.

Very little learning actually takes place in kids' karate classes because the young students have limited attention spans. They might pick up a little, but they have no idea why they're learning certain techniques. Realistically, you don't want them to learn too much at their age, or before long, karate will cease to be fun for them. They won't respond to a traditional, strict class and should not be expected to adhere to many of the rules.

Although classes must be fun, they also need to have some discipline. For example, it's important to have the young students tie their belts correctly. And they should call their instructor "sir" and learn how to bow correctly. They should be required to wear a *gi*—just as young baseball and football players are required to wear a uniform.

How do you select the right school for your 4- or 5-year-old? Go to the prospective school with your child and observe him. If he's excited about what he sees, that's a good sign.

Most kids will have more fun in a Korean-style class than in a Japanese-style class. In Korean classes, they will throw exciting kicks—like the roundhouse and jumping front kick—as opposed to the more basic kicks and exercises from the Japanese arts. They'll probably think that the Korean stylists are the closest thing to the fighters they see in movies and on television and will therefore probably enjoy learning those flashy styles.

An exception is judo, which is a Japanese art but also a good option for kids. The vast majority of judo involves throwing one's opponent, and the art is generally taught with a laid-back and playful manner that often appeals to young martial artists.

SHOW ME THE MONEY!

June 2000

The debate has gone on for decades: Should martial arts instructors charge for lessons or teach for free? Are instructors who charge somehow less devoted to the arts than those who don't? Are they money mongers or just average Joe's trying to earn an honest living?

I believe they're just trying to earn a living. There is absolutely nothing wrong with charging a fee for teaching a martial art, and it's ludicrous to say that anyone who charges a fee doesn't love the arts enough, and that if he did he'd teach out of the goodness of his heart.

Like most people who perform at seminars, I charge a fee, and it must be significant enough for me to travel to wherever the seminar is taking place. And I bet most people, except maybe for a few die-hards out there, would agree that there's nothing wrong with that.

If a student doesn't have enough money to pay for lessons, most instructors will accommodate him by assigning tasks around the dojo, such as mopping the floors.

You get what you pay for—in life and in the martial arts. Full-time teachers who charge a fee for lessons are normally more effective than part-timers who teach just a few hours a week. Full-timers elevate the status of the martial arts because they're able to convey high-quality information to their students. Whenever a professional has eight or 10 hours a day to devote to an endeavor, chances are he'll be able to perfect his skills and refine his art.

Even though there's a perception that some great instructors in Japan and other Far East nations don't get paid for teaching, for the most part it's not accurate. Wherever you go in the world, you'll find that most people get paid to teach the martial arts. It's not just the American way; it's the way of the world. Of course, if a student doesn't have enough money to pay for lessons, most instructors will accommodate him by assigning tasks around the *dojo*, such as mopping the floors.

These days, instructors seem concerned with maintaining student enrollment and selling martial arts merchandise—and rightfully so. Without these two sources of income, most would not be able keep their schools open. A school may seem to be raking in an exorbitant amount of money every month, but that can be deceiving. Operational expenses add up, and instructors don't pocket as much money as his students think.

One more point to consider: It's often true that students who take lessons for free fail to get as much out of training as students who pay. Those who are getting a free ride are more apt to skip class, and when they do attend, they don't put forth as much effort as those who pay.

When it comes to money, today's martial arts teachers are different from the teachers of 20 or 30 years ago. They're more interested in money than their '60s and '70s counterparts. What's wrong with that? The hard truth is that instructors have to be concerned with money or they'll go out of business. But that doesn't mean they should give up doing things that don't bring in an immediate profit—like giving a free lesson to a new student.

KICKBOXING THEN AND NOW

July 2000

Take a look at the competitors at any top-flight kickboxing venue. Watch how they move and try to imagine the resolve it took for them to get where they are. A question naturally arises: How is modern kickboxing different from the sport back in the '60s and '70s? As a champion from that period, I believe I'm qualified to make a few comments about fighting then and now.

First, it's true that kickboxers have evolved since the '70s. Today's fighters are more athletic and skilled, and they have better technique. However, in many cases, they lack the heart that the great fighters of yesteryear possessed. Back in the old days, if you wanted to be a winner, you had to knock your opponent out. Now, some kickboxers even say they don't want to fight that way anymore. And they tend to quit sooner than many of the old-timers. Often, they just seem to give up before anyone gets knocked out or the bell sounds.

Second, today's kickboxers have more time to practice because the money is much better. Back in the '60s and '70s, we were paid very little. Most of us had to maintain a regular job to supplement our martial arts activities. A big kickboxing match today might earn a competitor $100,000. The most I ever got paid for one fight was $7,500; no one could make a living on that paltry amount. Being able to earn a greater income means people can become full-time fighters.

Third, most of today's best fighters come from the Netherlands. Dutchmen Peter Aerts and Ernesto Hoost are two of the best. When I competed, kickboxing was more popular here than in Europe. However, it has really grown in popularity on the other side of the Atlantic, while it has remained stagnant, if not less popular, here in the United States. In the old days, Americans were among the most elite fighters in the world because we worked at it. But now, Europe is spawning the best fighters. The balance of power has shifted.

One specific way that Europe is influencing the international kickboxing scene involves the inclusion of leg kicks in bouts. They're great at kicking the legs; in fact, that's where they aim most of their shots. Europeans love leg kicks, but a lot of Americans consider them to be dirty fighting, and we generally don't like to see them used in the ring.

Many readers have asked how well I would do if I were competing in my prime against today's fighters. Although there's no way to say for sure, I like to think I'd do well. I had a lot of heart, and that's the most important thing. Plus, I had good endurance. When you have the heart and the endurance, the techniques will come. I think other champions of yesteryear would also do well; Benny "The Jet" Urquidez, Joe Lewis and Don "The Dragon" Wilson come to mind as fighters who would definitely be successful.

WHERE'S THE SPORTSMANSHIP IN TOURNAMENTS?
April 2001

It used to be that karate wasn't just about learning how to protect yourself; it also taught you how to get along with other people. These days, practitioners in *dojo* around the country still learn self-confidence and respect as they hone their martial arts techniques, but all those traits seem to go out the window at tournaments, where competitors frequently yell at referees when they don't like a particular call. Even competitors who have loads of self-confidence and skill become disrespectful jerks when they see their peers manipulate the rules and disrespect the officials. This does not represent what we strive to become.

Fighting etiquette started waning when the first competitor was awarded prize money for winning a tournament. It used to be that a fighter scored a point by throwing a controlled technique and pulling up short before the strike or kick landed and injured the opponent. Now, to score—and move one step closer to the cash—he needs to only touch his opponent. Furthermore, numerous regulations specify what a valid technique is.

Most tournaments use four judges and a referee to interpret and enforce the regulations. They try their best to judge fairly, but they can't see everything that goes on in a match, and whether a fighter receives a point or a penalty is often arbitrary. In fact, the competitors and spectators sitting ringside often see more than the judges do. When a fighter feels he's been cheated, he or his friends often shout at the judges to protest the "bad" call. Coaches and instructors can also enter the fray: If a student loses the tournament, he might quit karate and the coach will lose a student. That forces the instructor to do everything he can—including intimidate officials—to make sure his student gets the point.

It's legitimate for a fighter and his coach to protest a rule infraction, but even if a bad call is made against him, he should learn to relax. Chances are that he will also receive a couple of calls in his favor during the course of the fight, and things will balance out. And he should remember that it's usually his own fault if he gets a bad call because he was obviously close enough for the opponent to have scored a point in the first place.

But complaints about scoring are not the only examples of poor sportsmanship. Some fighters participate only in competitions they believe they can win. Their desire to bag a trophy outweighs their willingness to really test and improve their ability by fighting an equally skilled rival.

Other martial artists are as proficient at fighting as they are at manipulating the rules: They may claim that they need to fix their foot pads or that their hand came out of their glove so they can get 30 seconds of rest while they pretend to refasten their gear.

Fighting etiquette started waning when the first competitor was awarded prize money for winning a tournament.

None of this constitutes good sportsmanship. That's because for many people there is more at stake than winning a trophy or a title. Whereas it used to cost only $10 to $15 to enter a tournament, competitors now pay up to $50 to participate, and they want to get their money's worth. But real karate competition should not be about the money or the trophies. It's about enjoying yourself and knowing you fought to the best of your abilities.

BLACK BELT®
presents

THE ULTIMATE KICKING COLLECTION
Books and DVDs

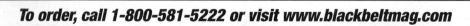